A Spiritual Autobiography

by

Michael Langford

www.seeseer.com

www.thefreedomreligionpress.com

ISBN: 978-1-937995-73-7

CONTENTS

INTRODUCTION

Manonasa is the final end of the ego-mind.
Manonasa is the final end of the false self.
When Manonasa occurs the ego-mind is dead forever.
Almost all of the words in a dictionary
point towards unreal illusions.
We will call that the human dream.

When Manonasa occurs
all of the following disappear forever
and can never reappear in all of eternity:

1. The human dream.
2. The ego-mind.
3. The false self.
4. All suffering.
5. All sorrow.

After Manonasa occurs what remains after
everything else has disappeared is:

Absolutely Perfect
Infinite Eternal Awareness-Love-Bliss.

Manonasa is extremely rare.
Less than one out of every five hundred million humans
attains Manonasa.

Less than 1 out of every 500,000,000 humans
attains Manonasa.

There are usually less than
twenty people living on the earth
at any one time who have attained Manonasa.
Manonasa is extremely rare.

There are thousands of
different types of spiritual experiences
that have been given thousands of different names
in many different spiritual teachings.
Almost none of those spiritual experiences
are Manonasa.

Only one who has attained Manonasa
has awakened.

All those who have not attained Manonasa
are still dreaming the human dream.

A biography or autobiography of one
who has attained Manonasa can be very helpful
to those few who would like to attain Manonasa
and those who are ready
or are on the brink of making the decision
to dedicate their lives to attaining Manonasa.

In this book the human before Manonasa
is M the seeker.
Just the letter M will be used to refer to M the seeker.
The post Manonasa appearance will be called Michael.
The post Manonasa Reality will be described in detail.

In this book the profound effect
that reading the biography of Ramana Maharshi
had on M will be described.
It completely changed the goal and direction of M's life.
That is the value of a biography or autobiography
of someone who has attained Manonasa.
It can change the Life of those few
who have somehow bypassed the ego-mind's deceptions
long enough to be open to the possibility
that Manonasa is the only worthwhile event
that can happen to a human.

If you were to survey 100,000 spiritual seekers
and ask them this question:

If someone says they have attained
the same enlightenment as the Buddha,
do you believe that is possible,
or do you think that
because they just made that claim
that proves they could not have attained
the same enlightenment as the Buddha?

Almost 100% of those surveyed would answer
that anyone who claims to have attained
the same enlightenment as the Buddha
could not have attained
the same enlightenment as the Buddha
because the very fact that they made that claim
proves that they have not attained
the same enlightenment as the Buddha.
They think that someone who had attained
the same enlightenment as the Buddha
would never make that claim.

All but one or two people out of the 100,000
would have that same view.
Spiritual seekers are like programmed robots
who follow such ideas
without ever wondering about their validity.

That commonly held idea
has no basis whatsoever.
There is no truth in the commonly held belief
that if someone claims to have attained
the same enlightenment as the Buddha
that means they have not attained
the same enlightenment as the Buddha.
That is a false belief.

The same applies to someone who claims
to have attained Self-Realization
or someone who claims to have attained Manonasa.
The same applies to someone who claims to be a Jnani
or someone who claims to be a Jivan-Mukta.
Yes a person **can** have attained Manonasa, Jnana,
Jivanmukta, Self-Realization or Nirvana **and say so**.
The ego-mind invented the idea that they cannot say so.

The reason it is almost never true
when people make such claims
is because Manonasa, etc. is so very rare.
If there are less than 20 people living on the planet
at any one time who have attained Manonasa, etc.
and there are 8,000 people either claiming directly or
implying indirectly that they have attained Manonasa
etc. then at least 7,980 people
are either deliberately lying or deluded or mistaken.

That is why such claims are almost never true.
Not because someone who has attained Manonasa
cannot state the fact that they have attained Manonasa.

The Buddha said
he had not attained the final enlightenment
until he had realized the Four Noble Truths.
That means the Buddha just told you
he has attained the final enlightenment.
It is not egotism for the Buddha to tell you
he has attained the final enlightenment.
The Buddha is just telling you the truth
when the Buddha tells you
he has attained the final enlightenment.
It is not egotism for the Buddha
to tell you what has happened.
It is true that he had attained the final enlightenment.
In that particular case the Buddha stated it directly.

However, if you include all the times
the Buddha *implied* that he had attained Nirvana,
the Buddha did that hundreds of times.
It was never egotism any of those hundreds of times.
The Buddha was just telling you the truth.

When Annamalai Swami was asked
if he was permanently established in the Self
Annamalai Swami said Yes.
It was not egotism for Annamalai Swami to say Yes.
Annamalai Swami was just telling you the truth.
Annamalai Swami was just stating a fact.

When Muruganar wrote an entire book
telling you about his experiences
and told you in hundreds of different ways
that he had attained the final Realization of the Self,
he was not being egotistical.
He was just telling you the truth.
He was just telling you what happened.
He was just stating the facts.

When Lakshmana Swami
described his Self Realization
in the book No Mind I Am The Self
it was not egotism.
Lakshmana Swami was just describing what happened.

When Papaji wrote about his own enlightenment
in his diary, Papaji was not being egotistical.
Papaji was just writing a fact.

When Nisargadatta Maharaj says
it only took him three years of practice
to realize the Self,
that means Nisargadatta Maharaj just told you
he has Realized the Self.

Nisargadatta was not being egotistical.
He was just stating a fact.
Nisargadatta is just stating the truth.
Nisargadatta is just telling you what happened.
The same applies to all of the different ways
that Nisargadatta communicated his state
like telling you he has no body,
and the talk is occurring in your world only.

When Michael says that in January of 2004
he attained Manonasa he is not being egotistical.
He is just telling you the truth.
He is just telling you what happened.
He is just stating a fact.

Would you like all those Sages to lie to you
and say that it did not happen,
just because almost every spiritual seeker believes
that those for whom it happened cannot say so?

Most people would answer that question no.
Most people would be lying.
Almost every spiritual teaching that has ever existed
in the history of humans has been for the purpose of
preserving the ego illusion.
Those teachings are not for the purpose of
ending the ego illusion.
That includes almost all of the spiritual teachings that
claim they are for the purpose of ending the ego illusion,
almost all of those teachings also are not really
for the purpose of ending the ego illusion.

Almost no human wants to end the ego illusion
even if they lie to themselves and think that they do
want to end the ego illusion.

The book you are now reading
is for that one in a million spiritual seeker
who is not following spiritual or other beliefs
he or she has accumulated in the past.
The book you are now reading is for that
one in a million spiritual seeker
in whom the desire to end the ego illusion
is actually greater than their desire
to preserve the ego illusion.
Not for spiritual seekers who are lying to themselves
believing the desire to end the ego illusion
is greater than the desire to preserve the ego illusion
when actually their desire to preserve the ego illusion
is greater than their desire to end the ego illusion.
When one understands
the thousands of layers of self deception
that all humans have, one knows that what those
thousands of layers of self deception want is to continue.
That is what almost all of the spiritual teachings
of the past are for, to preserve the ego illusion.
Almost all of the spiritual teachings of the past
are for the purpose of helping
the thousands of layers of self deception to continue.
All humans are lost dreaming the human dream.
All humans lie to themselves
from the time they wake up in the morning
until the time they go to sleep at night.

Most humans who read this book titled Manonasa
are going to reject the contents of this book.
This is known now before the book has been published.
This book states that
all of what has transpired so far in human history,
including the spiritual teachings of the past, is false.
Because humans are attached to their beliefs they are
going to view the contents of this book as false.

Humans
only see what the ego-mind allows humans to see.
The ego-mind is not going to allow most humans to see
the Truth of the contents of this book.
The contents of the book you are now reading
is going to cause a negative ego-reaction in most people.
Eventually there are going to be
many negative reviews of this book.
This is known now before this book has been published.
Humans are like a programmed machine.
If certain buttons are pushed
there will be a predictable negative reaction.

It would have been easy to
change the statements in this book
that are going to cause the most negative ego reaction.
That one in a million spiritual seeker in whom
the desire to end the impostor self
is greater than the desire to continue the impostor self
deserves a book with the Truth.
They deserve a book that does not change the contents
for the purpose of causing less of an ego reaction.
That one in a million spiritual aspirant
will love the contents of this book.
For them it will be like a breath of fresh air.
This book was written
for those one in a million spiritual aspirants.

The contents of this book have not been changed
to produce less of a negative ego reaction
in the majority of humans.

A small number of people
will see the great value in this book.
The majority will not see either the Truth or the value
of the contents of this book because all humans see
only what the impostor self allows them to see.

CHAPTER ONE

WHEN THE BODY WAS IN ITS CHILDHOOD YEARS

THE ABSENCE OF BIAS

The father of M's body was an atheist.
We will call the father of M's body B.
B believed that God was a fairy tale
and that all religion was false.
B was only familiar with the Christian religion
and no other religion, however,
B believed all religion was false
including the Christian religion
and including all the other religions
that B knew nothing about.

B had been raised in a Christian home.
B's mother went to church every Sunday.
B's mother was very much immersed
in her Christian Religion.
For example B's mother had
Matthew Henry's Commentary on the Whole Bible.
Not the concise version, the big version, all 5500 pages.
Yes, that is right, five thousand five hundred pages!

B also used to attend church
because he was raised that way.
B was a church band leader.
At some point when B's body was a teenager
B had seen enough hypocritical Christians
to sour him on all religion for the rest of his life
and make him an atheist for the rest of his life.
It was a long life, B's body passed away at age 89.

The mother of M's body was an agnostic.
Someone whose view is
they do not know if there is or is not a God.

The relevance of all this is that
there were no religious or spiritual books
in the home that M was raised in.
M was never taught anything about religion
and spirituality except that priests, ministers, etc.
were exploiting people.
This proved to be a great advantage.
When M studied more than 2000 books
from almost every spiritual path,
M was not biased towards any particular path.

If you were going to begin to list
what factors lead to Manonasa you could begin with:

Because M had never been taught
anything about any religious or spiritual path,
M was not biased towards any particular path when he
began to study almost all of the different spiritual paths.

People who are raised with
a particular spiritual path
are almost always biased towards
that type of spirituality.
Usually people are not aware of their bias
or how their bias is affecting their decisions.

BRIGHT AND MATURE

M was considered by most of the people
M came into contact with to be extremely intelligent
and mature for his body's age.
To give you a rough idea and a rough approximation
you could just double M's body age
and that is how M sounded to people.
For example when M's body was age five
M sounded like someone ten years old.
At body age 10 M sounded like someone
who had 20 years experience behind them.
At body age 15 M sounded like someone
who had 30 years experience behind them.

THE HOW DO I KNOW FOR SURE METHOD

When M's body was age 7,
M had a thought, an idea, a concept,
and a question arose:
"**How do I know for sure that is true**?"
The mind gave an answer
and to that answer the mind gave
M repeated the question:
"**How do I know for sure that is true**?"

M used that inquiry for thousands of ideas,
thoughts, beliefs and concepts
throughout M's childhood and teen years.
Every thought, idea, concept and belief ended with
"I don't know for sure this is true."

Sometimes the mind would keep giving answers
for ten or twenty times before the inquiry
finally ended in I don't know for sure this is true.

When M reached the teen years
M changed the question to:
"**How do I know absolutely for sure that is true**?"
Then later he switched back to
"**How do I know for sure that is true**?"
however, he always meant
"**How do I know absolutely for sure that is true**?"
by the question.

This inquiry throughout the childhood
and teen years made M realize that all thought's, ideas,
beliefs and concepts are baseless.
Thoughts, ideas, beliefs and concepts
were never able to get the firm hold on M that
they do on almost all humans because of this inquiry.
That made M very different from most humans.
If you are making a list of the factors
that ultimately led to Manonasa,
this *how do I know for sure* inquiry
throughout the childhood and teen years
was one of the factors.

M's approach was usually very different
than almost all human's approach.
It was **not** grace, magic, fate or luck that made M
one of those 1 in 500,000,000 humans
who attains Manonasa.
There were differences in M and M's approach.

M experienced a lot of suffering and sorrow
as a child.
That is because other children can sense someone
who is very different from them
and many children become very cruel
to that which is different.
Seeming twice as mature as his body's age,
made M very different.

That *how do I know for sure* inquiry
made M very different
because every human M ever came in contact with
was completely under the control of thoughts, ideas,
beliefs and concepts.
Due to the *how do I know for sure* inquiry,
M was only a little bit being controlled by thought.

That sorrow and suffering M experienced
as a child was the beginning of many motivations M had
to want to attain Manonasa.
There was much more suffering to come later
and that was also a motivating factor.
One of the motivating factors
had nothing to do with what M experienced directly.
Becoming aware of the vast ocean of evil
called 6 billion humans including their history
was also a great motivating factor for M
to want to attain Manonasa
and thus awaken from the human dream.

From body age 5 to 8 once per week
M would go to one of the movie theaters
that B owned and watch a movie.
Usually M would watch the movie from the seats.
Sometimes M would watch the movie
from the projection booth.
Seeing the projector and how a movie is projected onto
the screen etc. was a valuable spiritual lesson for M.
After M attained Manonasa, Michael began teaching,
and wrote many teaching examples and stories
that used various aspects of a movie theater.
Michael was thinking of that specific movie theater
M had been going to once per week
from body age 5 to body age 8
when writing the details of those stories and examples.

When M's body was age 11
M was having a conversation
with M's maternal grandmother.
The grandmother told M:
"When you talk to other people it is very important
that you never tell the people a lie."

M replied to the grandmother:

"**Even more important
than not lying to other people
is not lying to yourself**."

M had never been taught that.
M had been observing human behavior closely even
as a child and saw how the human mind lies to itself.
Most humans go their whole lives unaware of the fact
that they are lying to themselves every day of their lives.
At age 11 M had seen
one of the most important spiritual lessons that exist.
A lesson that most humans never see
throughout their whole lives.
That includes almost every spiritual seeker also.
Almost no spiritual seeker sees
that they are lying to themselves every day.
If there is a rare one who does see that
almost all of those continue
to lie to themselves every day.

Even at body age 11 M was quite unique.
M had seen the importance of not lying to yourself
and that people were continually lying to themselves.
Even at body age 7 M was quite unique due to the
how do I know for sure inquiry.

CHAPTER TWO

WHEN THE BODY WAS IN ITS TEEN YEARS

When M's body was age 13, 14, and 15 M was
spending a lot of time reading books on psychology,
going to encounter and other types of groups
led by famous psychologists,
studying the human potential teachings and
Transactional Analysis, Gestalt Therapy, hypnosis, etc.

When M's body was age 15
M had never read even one religious or spiritual book.
When M's body was age 15 close to the age 16 birthday,
M was in a bookstore.
For some reason instead of going
to the psychology section like he usually did
he went to where the alternative (non Christian)
spiritual books were.

M bought a book titled
The Spiritual Teachings of Ramana Maharshi
published by Shambala.
That changed the course of M's life.
The notion that one might not be the body, mind, etc.
and that *instead* of having a *belief* about the true Self
one could have the *direct experience* of the true Self
was fascinating to M.

The question Who Am I being asked,
without allowing thoughts, ideas, concepts, beliefs
or opinions to answer the question,
since the only true answer is in the
direct experience of the Infinite Self,
also fascinated M.

At body age 16 and 17
M read around 50 Ramana Maharshi books.
Most of those were books he had ordered
from Sri Ramanasramam.

There were four books M bought at bookstores
in the USA:

1. *The Spiritual Teachings of Ramana Maharshi*,
published by Shambala.

The following three books published by Samuel Weiser:

2. *The Teachings of Ramana Maharshi*
by Arthur Osborne.

3. *The Collected Works of Ramana Maharshi.*

4. *Ramana Maharshi and the Path of Self Knowledge*
by Arthur Osborne which was a biography
of Ramana Maharshi.

That biography of Ramana Maharshi
had a profound effect on M.
B (the father of M's body) had said
that all spiritual and religious leaders
were exploiting people.
The more that M learned about
the life of Ramana Maharshi,
the more M realized that
Ramana Maharshi was 100% authentic
and M could see that Ramana Maharshi
was not exploiting people

Here are some examples of what made it clear
to M that Ramana Maharshi was authentic
and not exploiting people:

After arriving at Arunachala
there was a period of time when
Ramana Maharshi was so absorbed in the Self that:
Ants were eating Ramana Maharshi's body
and Sri Ramana
continued to remain absorbed in the Self.
No one who is putting on some act
is going to remain still and absorbed
while ants are eating his body.
Everyone else would do something to stop the ants.
M could see that here was someone truly different.
Ramana Maharshi was obviously 100% True
and 100% Authentic
and Ramana Maharshi had no selfishness
that exploits people.
There is an expression in America
"This is the real deal."

There are so many examples.
Here are some other examples:
one time Ramana Maharshi
and some other people there at Sri Ramanasramam
were drinking coffee.
There was not enough coffee for everyone.
When Ramana Maharshi realized
that he had been drinking coffee
when there was not enough coffee
for everyone who wanted coffee:
Ramana Maharshi
never had one sip of coffee again in his life!

After Ramana Maharshi arrived at Arunachala
he threw away the little money he had left and then:
Ramana Maharshi
never touched money again for the rest of his life!
Eventually Ramana Maharshi
had thousands of devotees
and if he wanted to live in luxury he could have.
He lived in just the opposite of luxury.
Ramana Maharshi had a very sparse lifestyle.
Ramana Maharshi's only possessions were
a walking stick, a water pot, a loin cloth and a towel!
People were constantly giving Ramana Maharshi gifts.
Ramana Maharshi returned all the gifts!

This all made such an impression on M's mind.
Suppose there are one million spiritual teachers.
And 999,999 of those spiritual teachers are phonies
who still have an ego.
If there is a one out of a million exception
it means that not all are phonies.
Ramana Maharshi was that one in a million exception.
Ramana Maharshi had no girlfriend or wife!
That was very impressive to M also
because it meant that Ramana Maharshi's motivations
were very different from the motivations of a human.
It also meant that all the talk about Bliss and inner joy
was true.

Ramana Maharshi
had a different source of joy than a human has.
There were many other things that
M read about in Ramana Maharshi's life
that made a strong impression on M.
Ramana Maharshi never ate meat, eggs or fish.

Being aware of Ramana Maharshi's authentic behavior,
sort of a saintly or saint like behavior,
can serve a great purpose
for the type that M the seeker was.
And it did serve a great purpose for M the seeker.
At the young body age of 15
M the seeker changed the purpose of his life.
The purpose was now to realize the Self.
The authentic behavior of Ramana Maharshi
can serve a great purpose for many spiritual seekers.
However, it only serves the best purpose
for certain types of spiritual seeker.

There is another factor regarding the impression Ramana Maharshi made on M.
Ramana Maharshi's infinite wisdom
came from the direct experience of the infinite,
not from beliefs, theories, ideas, concepts, opinions, etc.

The fact that almost all spiritual and religious teachers are exploiting those who read or listen to them
is only one of the reasons why
those very rare seekers of Truth will reject them.
The other reason is that
almost none of those spiritual and religious teachers
are living from the infinite True Self.
Almost all of those religious and spiritual teachers
have collected spiritual or religious ideas, beliefs,
opinions, concepts, etc.
and are now passing all of that garbage
unto those who read them or who listen to them.
Humans love to put garbage into their minds.
The reason spiritual and religious teachers are almost always teaching garbage is because garbage is what humans demand and garbage is what humans crave.

All humans are controlled by those thousands of layers
of self deception and those thousands of layers of
self deception feed on garbage and grow from garbage.
If the thousands of spiritual and religious books that
have been written in the past were honest the title of
those books would be ______ *Pages of Garbage.*
i.e. *200 Pages of Garbage.*
150 Pages of Garbage.
700 Pages of Garbage.

Before M's body reached age 18
he had read more than 50 Ramana Maharshi books.
M was open to what he was reading.
There was a complete receptiveness
to what M was reading.
Thus reading those books
completely changed the Goal of M's life.

M had been raised by a man (B)
who had been self employed since age 18.
M's conversations with B from childhood onward
were almost always about business, money,
investments, real estate, etc.
M's goal prior to age 15
was to become the richest man in the world.
Although M's goal changed
from the very first time he read the book
The Spiritual Teachings of Ramana Maharshi
it took a couple of years for M to learn how to
center his entire life around the goal of Self Realization.
When M read the biography
Ramana Maharshi and the Path of Self Knowledge
at body age 16 or 17,
that produced the final change in M's view
that motivated M to drop everything from his life
that was not contributing to Realizing the Self.

The combination of that
and the other 50 Ramana Maharshi books
that M had read before body age 18
had produced a mind whose view was
that there is only one goal worthwhile in life
and that goal is
to have the direct experience of the True Self
and to remain absorbed in the True Self
until Manonasa occurred.

Reading that biography of Ramana Maharshi
allowed M to see that some beings are
impeccable in their behavior.
From body age 18 onward M's behavior
was always impeccable
and the hope is that reading this autobiography of M
will allow people to see that even though
Manonasa is extremely rare
and the combination of Manonasa
and impeccable behavior is even more rare,
such beings continue to arise.

In the future also,
for thousands of years in the future
humans will attain Manonasa.
In the far distant future Manonasa will not be as rare
as it has been in the past.
In the far distant future humans will see the value
of the 20 steps to Manonasa
that are listed at the end of this book.
For now most humans will not see that.
Most humans are going to reject
the contents of the book you are now reading.
This is known now,
even before the book has been published.
Humans see only what the ego wants them to see.
In the future humans will see the value of this book.

At body age 15 M had a "girlfriend."
Her body was one year older than M's body.
At body age 17 M was living with the girlfriend.
Before body age 18 M asked the girlfriend to move out.
M had made a decision that having a girlfriend
took time, energy, and attention.
M wanted all of that time, energy and attention
to be directed to realizing the Self.

M never had a girlfriend again.
M never had a wife.
The last time M's body had physical relations
with another human being
was when M's body was age 17.
The reason decades later M attained Manonasa
was **not** grace, luck, fate, destiny or magic.
It was because M's approach was different.
From the beginning of this book
the ways in which M's approach was different
have been described.
Someone who was interested in
being one of those extremely rare
one in five hundred million humans who attain
Manonasa would have been circling the passages
in this book from the beginning of this book
describing how M's approach was different
from most humans and what were the factors
that led to M eventually attaining Manonasa.

Another description
of how M's approach was different
is that M's desire was so strong to Realize the Self
and attain Manonasa,
M dropped everything that is unnecessary from his life
in order to free up the maximum amount of time
so that the freed up time could be directed towards
the goal of Self Realization and attaining Manonasa.

Never having physical relations, or a girlfriend
or a wife after body age 17 is one example
of M dropping all that is unnecessary from M's life.

When a male body is in its teens
and twenty's the amount of desire
for physical relations is intense.
It took an iron will
to never have any physical relations again.
When the body was in its twenties
so many woman looked so attractive.
There were two things that allowed M to succeed
in his vow never to have physical relations again.
One was the intense desire for Freedom
or in other words the intense desire for Self Realization.
The other was that M thought about
all the men in human history who had succeeded
in ceasing to have physical relations
for the sake of their spiritual development.
When you add up all of the Sannyasins
from what the west calls Hinduism,
all of the Buddhist Monks,
and all of the Christian Monks
who have succeeded
in never again having physical relations
for the sake of their spiritual development
the total is millions of men who have succeeded.
M knew that since millions of men had succeeded
in never again having physical relations
for the sake of their spiritual development,
that he too could succeed
in never again having physical relations.
Most people focus on the men
who try such a vow and fail.
A sannyasin, a Buddhist monk,
a Christian monk, a priest
who attempts such a vow and fails.

This shows you how sick the human mind is.
Humans get a thrill out of thinking about
those who tried such a vow and failed.
Most people never think about all the millions of men
who have tried such a vow and succeeded.
It took a huge amount of will power
when M's body was in its twenties to keep that vow.
When M's body was in its twenties
there was very much desire for those physical relations.
M's mind was telling M
that having those physical relations
was as necessary as breathing.
M's mind was lying,
the body will not live without breath.
The body can live without those physical relations.
M was 100% successful in keeping his vow.
After body age 17
M never again had any physical relations.
At the moment Manonasa occurred in January of 2004
all desire for physical relations disappeared
and it has never returned.
Since January of 2004
there has not even been one second
when Michael had any desire for physical relations.

When people authentically devote their lives
to spiritual awakening
a flood of miraculous events happen.

Here is a story we can call Sri Ramana's Grace:

When M's body was in its teens
in Las Vegas Nevada in the 1970's,
his interest and attention was on
the teachings of Sri Ramana Maharshi.
M had not met anyone in Las Vegas
who had even heard of Sri Ramana Maharshi.

One day M was on his way home
driving on Las Vegas Blvd. (the Las Vegas Strip)
and M saw an elderly Indian couple
waving at him, obviously wanting M to stop.
M stopped and they told M
they wanted to go to the airport.
So M drove them to the airport.
At that time M had a personalized
Nevada License Plate that said "RAMANA."
M asked them "is the reason that you waved at me to
stop because you saw my 'RAMANA' license plate?"
The wife told M
"No, we did not see your Ramana license plate.
We thought you were a taxi.
If we had known you were not a taxi,
we would not have accepted the ride."
The husband told M he had met Sri Ramana Maharshi
when he was a young man.
He had some doubts and he told them to Sri Ramana,
and Sri Ramana cleared his doubts.
The wife looked surprised.
Even she did not know that her husband
had gone to see Sri Ramana Maharshi
when he was young.
So there is an example both of
Sri Ramana's grace and a miraculous event.
M had not even met someone
who had heard of Sri Ramana Maharshi
and now M was talking to someone
who had actually met Sri Ramana.
If the setting had been India in the 1970's
that may not have been that surprising
to have met someone who had spoken with Sri Ramana.
However, this was Las Vegas, Nevada - USA.
A city known for Casino's, not spirituality.

The place where the couple waved at M
was vacant land back in the 1970's.
Now on that same land there is a famous hotel
called the Luxor that is shaped like a pyramid
and they have a huge replica – statue of the sphinx
very near where M picked that couple up.
The miraculous part of this event
was not only meeting someone
who had met Sri Ramana.
The big question is what made that Indian couple
wave at M to stop?

The wife said, if we had known you were not a
taxi, we would not have accepted the ride.
The car M was driving was a Ford LTD.
The Ford LTD was a huge rectangular shaped car
with very square edges.
M's car was dark brown, a similar color to chocolate.
M's huge car did not look anything like
an American taxi or an Indian taxi.
Therefore, what made that couple see a taxi?
The wife said they would not have accepted the ride
if they had known you were not a taxi.
What made them see a taxi in a car
that looks nothing like a taxi and that was not a taxi?
Thus through Sri Ramana's grace
M was able to meet someone
who had met and spoken with Sri Ramana,
right there in Las Vegas.
You can imagine how thrilling that was
for a young man whose attention was
so focused on the teachings of Sri Ramana.
The couple wanted to pay M for the ride.
M would not accept any money.
They had already paid M a fortune
by allowing M to meet someone
who had actually met Sri Ramana.

At body age 17
M did a six month experiment with honesty.
M wanted to be as honest as a human being could be.
That included both honesty with other people
and self honesty.
If M thought there had been an exaggeration
in what he had said to another person,
M would tell that other person that was an exaggeration,
the truth is____________.

One day during this six month experiment
with honesty M went into a grocery store
to purchase some hamburger meat.
The hamburger meat package
had a white Styrofoam bottom
and the top was clear plastic
so that people could see the meat.
M looked at that hamburger meat
and asked himself this question:
"If I had to do what it took
to get this hamburger meat into this package,
could I still eat the hamburger meat?"
M realized the answer to that question was **no**
he could **not** eat the hamburger meat
if he had to do what it took to get that hamburger meat
into that package.
M realized that if he ate the hamburger meat
he would be lying to himself.
M realized that if he ate the hamburger meat
he would be ignoring what had to happen
to get the hamburger meat into that package
or pretending that what had to happen
to get the hamburger meat into that package
had not happened.

M did not buy that hamburger meat.
From that moment onward,
M never had another bite of meat, eggs or fish
in his entire life.

M had a deep insight regarding eating meat.
Because of the deep insight M did not have to use
any discipline or effort to stop eating meat.
From the moment of that insight forward
M had no desire to eat meat, eggs or fish.
From the moment of that insight forward
M found even the thought of eating meat, eggs or fish
repulsive.

On the day of the insight M thought about
what if M had raised the cow since the cow's birth.
And watched the cow grow up.
After the cow was grown up could M kill the cow,
then take the cows skin off,
then cut up the cows dead body.
Then take pieces of the cows dead body
grind it up and put it in a package,
and then could M eat the meat?
M realized in that deep insight the answer was **NO**.
If M had to do all that he could **not** eat the meat.
M realized that if he ate the meat
after someone else had done all that,
M would be lying to himself.

From body age 18 until body age 38
M operated the family business,
a small 26 unit motel on the strip in Las Vegas.
When M was going to begin his work at the Motel,
M had the opportunity to write his own work schedule.
In other words what hours and on what days
M would be working the front desk at the motel.

M had just learned that Vernon Howard
had classes in Boulder City.
Boulder City was around a 30 or 35 minute drive
from where M lived.

Vernon Howard had four classes per week.
Even though M had never been to a
Vernon Howard class
M wrote his work schedule
so that he would be able to attend
all four classes every week.
The work schedule needed to be written immediately
and there was no time to first attend
a Vernon Howard class
before deciding if he wanted to continue.

One would never know
what Vernon Howard was like
from reading one of Vernon Howard's books.

If you listen to many recordings
of Vernon Howard's classes
then you can get some idea of what he was like
if you pay attention to the tones of voice he used,
the raising of his voice and the content of what he said.

M attended Vernon Howard's classes
four times per week for three months.
M never missed a class.
Seeing Vernon Howard in person
was like expecting to see a spiritual teacher sitting in
that chair and what you see sitting in the chair is a Lion.
The Lion often would roar and seem very angry.

M once asked Vernon Howard
“**Is the purpose of this class
to remove the illusion of the ego**?”
Vernon asked M to repeat the question.
M repeated the question and Vernon answered
“Yes. Well stated.”

M once asked Vernon Howard
“**Is it possible to use your teachings
to preserve the ego instead of to end the ego**?”
Vernon answered “**Yes, and you all do it**.”

Thus from that question one can see that
at body age 18 M had already seen that
even with teachings that are for the purpose
of bringing the ego illusion to its final end,
the ego can change and distort the teachings
and use the teachings in a way
that will help to make the ego illusion continue,
instead of bringing the ego illusion to its final end.

From age 18 onward
M never made any new friendships
and M never had any hobbies.
The reason is because that would have used up time
that could have been directed towards Self Realization.
M only had one goal in life from body age 18 onwards.
That goal was to bring the ego-illusion to its final end
and to directly experience the true Self.
From body age 18 onward,
all of M’s life was directed to the one goal.

CHAPTER THREE

WHEN THE BODY WAS IN ITS TWENTIES

Maybe around the year 1980, give or take a year,
when M's body was around 21 years old,
M went to Oakland, California
to the Siddha Yoga Ashram
while Swami Muktananda was there.
The ashram schedule had long days.
Meditation was at around 4:00 AM or 5:00 AM.

There was one or another type of chanting or
singing going on from around 6:00 AM until 10:00 PM
with the exception of a two hour Guruseva period
where one did some volunteer work.
Even during lunch etc. the chanting would continue
Sri Ram Jai Ram....

During that month there was one Intensive.
The Intensive was on a weekend,
a Saturday and a Sunday.
Two times on Saturday and two times on Sunday
Muktananda would touch each person in the Intensive
individually.
He did not use his hands to touch the person.
He used peacock feathers.

All four times when Muktananda touched M
light exploded in M's mind.
This was very unusual for M
because M almost never had any experiences of light
in the mind.

Just before the second time
Muktananda was going to touch M,
M put his hands over his eyes.
The reason M did that is because
M was suspicious that maybe they had a device
that directed a very powerful beam of light
towards people's eyes.
So that even though people had their eyes closed,
they would see light.
Putting the hands over the eyes
did not make any difference.
The same light exploded once again at the moment
Muktananda touched M for the second time.
The reason light was experienced was because
it was one of Muktananda's Siddhis (powers)
to be able to make light explode in people's minds.

The reason M was suspicious of a device
was because they charged $150 for the Intensive.
500 people attended the Intensive.
500 x $150 = $75,000.
That is Seventy Five Thousand dollars.
That is a huge sum of money.
If you adjusted that for inflation,
that would be a much higher sum today
because around 35 years has passed.

There were some times when M was chanting
Om Namah Shivaya with his eyes closed
at the Siddha Yoga Ashram
when M experienced a flickering light in the mind.

One day M was sitting in the area
where one takes one's shoes off.
The meditation hall was on the other side
of big double doors.
Light was appearing in M's mind.

M went into the meditation hall and
Swami Muktananda was sitting there all by himself.
His power had gone right through the door.
The power of suggestion is eliminated from this
because M had no idea Swami Muktananda
was sitting in the meditation hall
because there was nothing scheduled.

One time M was drinking from a water fountain
in a hallway there at the Siddha Yoga Ashram.
M started to experience a huge amount of joy.
Thinking it had something to do with the water,
M continued to drink the water.
Suddenly Muktananda appeared
at the other end of the hallway.
The power of suggestion is eliminated
because M had no idea that Muktananda
was about to appear at the other end of the hallway.

When I say appear,
I just mean that Muktananda was in another room
and left the other room and walked into the hallway.
All of these encounters with Muktananda
were with Muktananda physically present,
not some mysterious appearance.

In both the hallway incident
and the meditation hall incident
Muktananda and M were alone.
M was lucky to have that happen.
Usually there were five hundred other people present
whenever M saw Muktananda.

There at the same time
that M was there at the Siddha Yoga Ashram
there was a man named Leonard
who happened to be staying
at the same ashram run guest house M was staying in.
Muktananda gave Leonard the name Mahesh.

M had driven his Ford Ltd
with a customized license plate that said RAMANA
from Las Vegas to Oakland.
Of course the RAMANA was for Ramana Maharshi.

Leonard was from a country called
Trinidad/Tobago.
They did not have many spiritual book stores
there in Trinidad/Tobago.
This was in the days before Amazon.com
or the internet existed.
Leonard asked M would he drive Leonard around
to various spiritual bookstores.
M said yes and M spent a day driving Leonard
around to various spiritual bookstores in San Francisco.

One of the bookstores was called Fields.
A very famous spiritual bookstore with a huge selection
of eastern spiritual books.

M was not very interested in buying books
that day.
Mostly M just wanted to provide transportation
for Leonard so that he could buy books.
There at Fields there was the original hard cover
two volume edition of the Yoga Vasistha that
Swami Venkatesananda had translated into English.
Leonard was looking at one of the volumes.
Leonard told M that M should buy it.

M was not interested in buying books that day.
Leonard was very insistent.
Leonard was telling M about how great the book is.
That was not enough to convince M,
so Leonard said to M
just read a little bit out of this book.
Leonard handed M one of the volumes.
M could see it immediately.
M could see that this was indeed
a very special spiritual book.
After all, M's orientation was the Path of Knowledge.
This was a two volume set about the Path of Knowledge.

M bought that two volume set immediately!
Those carefully selected Yoga Vasistha quotes
in the book *The Seven Steps to Awakening*
that appeared decades later,
all date back to that day when Leonard told M
to read something from the Yoga Vasistha.

In two different years in the 1980's,
it might have been 1984 and 1985
when M's body was age 25 and 26,
M attended J. Krishnamurti's series of Talks
in Ojai, California.
Each series of Talks lasted two weeks.
Talks were on the weekends
and question and answer sessions
were on the weekdays.

More than one thousand people
would attend each talk.
People arrived very early to get a good seat.
M arrived earlier to be the first or second in line
so that he could sit closer to Krishnamurti.

M was very quiet.
However, the crowd would be chattering away
the whole time from the time they arrived
until Krishnamurti arrived.

A thousand people chattering is very loud.
When people saw Krishnamurti's Mercedes arrive
the word spread quickly that he had arrived
and the crowd stopped chattering.
From the great thunder of more than 1000 people
chattering to everyone being quiet.

When Krishnamurti's Talk had ended
Krishnamurti would ask everyone to get up
and everyone except for one person in the crowd
would get up and leave.
The crowd would chatter again as they were leaving.

The one person who did not get up and leave
was M.
M stayed with his eyes shut for the purpose of reflecting
on what Krishnamurti had just said.

When M was attending the Talk, etc.
without having brought anyone with him
he would always stay there for a very long time
after the crowd had left,
usually for more than one hour.

Years earlier M had heard Krishnamurti
on a recording saying to the crowd
who was attending one of his talks:

"**Have you listened?**
No you have not listened
because if you had listened
you would have left here with ecstatic mind."

M remembered what Krishnamurti had said
and years later when M had the opportunity
to hear Krishnamurti Talk in person
M stayed there in the Oak Grove
(the place where Krishnamurti gave his Talks)
for a very long time reflecting on what Krishnamurti
had said that day
instead of letting the mind go on to other matters.

One time M brought the father of his body
to one of the weekend Talks.
Another time M brought the mother of his body
to one of Krishnamurti's Talks.
Another time M brought the ex-girlfriend
to one of Krishnamurti's Talks.

When M had brought someone to the Talk
with him he did not stay for long after
Krishnamurti's Talks
because that would be like trying to force the person
he had brought with him
to do something they did not want to do.

However, the people M brought with him
only attended a Talk for a day or two.
Therefore, out of the 4 weeks of Talks
in the two different years,
most of the time M attended the Talks alone
without having brought anyone with him.

Every time M attended a Talk, etc.
without having brought anyone with him
he always stayed for a very long time
after everyone else had left.
Usually M stayed for more than one hour
after everyone else had left.

When M would finally open his eyes
it was a strange sight not to see one other human being
there in the Oak Grove when before there had been
more than one thousand people there.

When Krishnamurti asked the people to get up
the entire crowd would get up
and it took them only around ten minutes
for all of them to have left the Oak Grove.

It was so nice that during the time
M was sitting there all alone
reflecting on what Krishnamurti had said
he did not have to listen to that crowd chattering.
If Krishnamurti had not asked everyone to get up
many people would have stayed there and chattered.

What one can see from what has been written
so far in this book
is that M had a very different approach
than everyone else's approach.

To not let the mind go on to other thoughts
and other activities
was a completely different approach
than the rest of the crowd was using.
The reason M had a very different approach
is because M's desire to Realize the Self
and bring the ego to its final end was very strong.

If you wonder is it by grace, luck, fate or magic
that those very few who attain Manonasa
(the final end of the false self
after which it can never reappear)
succeed in attaining Manonasa?
It is not by grace, luck, fate or magic.
It is by using a different approach than the crowd uses.

M's approach, M's views, M's methods were very
different and M's results were very different also.
All of what is written in this book
is for the purpose of conveying something to you.

The intensity of the desire for freedom
from the false self is the key factor.
When that desire for freedom
becomes extremely intense it changes everything.
The extremely intense desire for freedom
changes all of one's actions,
it increases the level of self honesty,
it changes one's approach to everything
and especially it changes one's approach to
how to go about attaining Manonasa.

It was **not** grace, fate, luck or magic
that led M to attain Manonasa.
It was the extremely intense desire
to bring the false self to a final end
that led M to attain Manonasa.

What makes one one of those
one in five hundred million humans
who attains Manonasa is:

1. An extremely intense desire
to bring the false self to its final end.
That desire eventually has as much energy
as a trillion stars.

2. An extremely intense level of self honesty.
That self honesty eventually
has as much energy as a trillion stars.

3. Dropping all unnecessary activities
and using all of the free time thus created
to practice the most direct and rapid means
to Manonasa.

It is **not** grace, it is **not** luck, it is **not** destiny,
and it is **not** magic that leads one to become
one of those one in five hundred million humans
who attains Manonasa.
It is the three items just listed
that leads one to attain Manonasa.

Regarding the fact that it is not magic,
consider this quote by Nisargadatta Maharaj:

"**Everyone does the same mistake,
wanting the ends but refusing the means.
We do not dispense magic here**!"

The crowd follows certain patterns.
In the case of J. K's Talks, etc.
the crowd used every second of time
before K showed up to chatter
and as soon as K was finished talking
they immediately began to chatter again.

If you think they were chattering about
what K just said,
then you don't know much about humans.
They were chattering about nonsense.
"What are we going to have for lunch?"

K has given an invitation to leave
with ecstatic mind
and the humans are thinking and chattering about:
"What are we going to have for lunch?"

The entire crowd got up and left
instead of staying and reflecting on what K had just said
while what K said was still fresh in mind.

Thoughts, beliefs, ideas, concepts, opinions, etc.
are also like a crowd that follows patterns.

After M finally did get up
he would always go to visit a white horse
that was in a nearby corral.
It was around a 5 or 10 minute walk
from the Oak Grove to the Corral.
M would rub the horse's nose and talk to the horse.
The horse enjoyed that because
the horse had a big corral
and the horse could have gone anywhere else
in that corral if it had not been enjoying that.
From wherever the horse was in that corral
the horse saw M and came up to the place
where M was standing and put his nose up to the fence
so that M could rub the horse's nose
and talk to the horse.

When you talk to animals,
you should always use a soft, soothing tone.
You should never make sudden movements
around animals.
A fast movement of your hand
could easily scare an animal.

The first point to be understood
is during and after the Talk, etc.
do not go on to some other thinking
or some other subject.
Do not get lost in something else.

That means to stay with what Krishnamurti
(or whatever Sage you are listening to)
just said in the Talk he just gave.

After the Talk, etc. is over keep asking yourself:
"What did K just say?"

From the second the Talk, etc. is over
continue keeping your mind on the Talk, etc.
The mind may wander unto something else
for a few seconds and if it does that it is OK
just bring it right back to the question:
"What did K just say in the Talk he just gave?"

Every time the mind wanders for a few seconds
unto something else bring it back to the question:
"What did K just say in his Talk?"
That is the first point and the primary point.

Even if you do not reflect,
keep bringing the mind back to that same question:
"What did K just say in his Talk?"

Bring what he just said back to mind.
That means you are keeping your mind on it
and not letting it go elsewhere.
For at least one hour after the Talk, etc. has ended
keep your mind on the question:
"What did K just say in his Talk?"

Be very careful about
what thought does at that point
because thought may invent an interpretation
of what K just said that is **not** what K just said.

The fact that someone did not go on to other thoughts
and thus get lost in other thoughts and subjects,
like the entire crowd did, is a great first step.

Just being willing to give up an extra 60 minutes
of your time after the Talk, etc. has ended
for the purpose of staying focused
on what was just said is a great first step.

If thought tries to add some interpretation
of what K just said ask yourself:
"Was this really what K just said
or is this some interpretation of what K just said?"

This example of K can be applied elsewhere.
You are reading one of those very rare spiritual books
that actually has the purpose of
leading people to Manonasa.
When thought comes in ask yourself:
"**Is this really what is written here,
or am I adding an interpretation
to what is written here**?"

There may be hundreds of different thoughts
that the crowd went unto next.
What all those different thoughts
on different subjects had in common
is that they had nothing to do with what K just said.

The greater the desire for freedom
the less likely that one will move on
to some other thought.

The greater the desire for freedom
the less likely that one will add some interpretation
to what a Sage writes or says.

Although there can be many different types
of thought the crowd went unto next,
beginning as soon as K's Talk, etc. ended,
the example used in the story was
"What are we going to have for lunch?"

There is a time and place where the question
"What are we going to have for lunch?"
is a good question to ask.

It is not a good question to ask when K
or any other Sage has just finished their Talk.
What is good at that moment is to ask yourself
"What did_____ just say in his or her Talk?"
And be willing to stay with that question
for more than one hour after the Talk has ended.

When M got up to go see the horse
M was no longer thinking about "What did K just say?"
If M had wanted to continue that inquiry
then it would have been best to just continue
to stay seated in the Oak Grove.

Once the decision was made
that there had been enough of the inquiry
"What did K just say?"
then the thought "What is next?" is appropriate.

For M what was next was to visit the horse.
On the way to visiting the horse the thought was about
walking in the direction of the horse.
The thought was not about K's Talk then.

After arriving at the corral
the attention was directed towards the horse,
not towards "What did K just say?"

If the thoughts had been about
"What did K just say?" when visiting the horse
that would demonstrate very little caring
about the horse and about what K had said
because that is divided attention:
part on the horse and part on what K said.

When reflecting on what K said,
that deserves undivided attention.
When visiting the horse,
the horse deserves undivided attention.
The horse is a living being who deserves kindness
and undivided attention.
Talking in a soft, kind, loving tone to the horse.
Rubbing the horse's nose.
Just M and the horse.
No thoughts about anything else.

If the horse goes to some other part
of the corral do not follow the horse.
Let the horse have his preference not to visit.

In this case the horse saw M approach the fence
and the horse came from wherever he was in the corral
right up to where M was standing
and pressed his nose through the fence
so that M could rub his nose.

After finishing visiting the horse
M probably thought about "What will I have for lunch?"
just like the crowd did.
The difference is **when** that thought was focused on.
After giving the question "What did K just say?"
M's undivided attention for an hour after the Talk
had ended, and after finishing visiting the horse,
not while visiting the horse, then the thought
"What shall I have for lunch?" probably occurred.

At that time the thought is appropriate.
The body needs food and "What shall I have for lunch?"
is a good question at the right time.

Someone might wonder maybe the reason
people did not stay and reflect on what K had said
is the same reason why M did not stay and reflect
when M went to the Talks with other people.
Because just like M they did not want
to be forcing the people they were with
to do what they did not want to do.

It may well be the same reason,
however, consider this;
let us suppose that out of the more than
one thousand people attending K's Talk
300 came alone and 700 came with other people.
Out of those 300 people, why did not one other person
stay in the Oak Grove to reflect on what K said
while what K said was still fresh in mind?
Having come alone those 300 people
did not need to be worried
if the other people they came with
would want to sit there
and reflect on what K just said.

Most of the series of Talks
and questions and answers for both years
M attended alone
without having brought anyone with him.
During all of those times when M attended alone,
not one other person stayed in the Oak Grove
to reflect on what K had just said
while it was still fresh in mind.

A very strong desire for Freedom
produces different actions, and a different approach.
A very strong desire for Freedom
in the end produces different results also.

The crowd never attains Manonasa.
Less than one out of every five hundred million humans
attains Manonasa.
This book from the beginning has been showing you
the difference in approach between
one who eventually attained Manonasa and those who
8,000,000,000,000,000,000,000
imaginary lifetimes from now
will still **not** have attained Manonasa
and will still be under the illusion
of the false ego-mind.

The reason why it matters
is because during those
8,000,000,000,000,000,000,000
future imaginary lifetimes
they are going to experience
the equivalent of 4,000,000,000,000
oceans of suffering and sorrow.
I want to save as many people as possible
from having to experience all of that
huge amount of suffering and sorrow.
This book you are now reading
is one of the Teachings I have created
for the purpose of saving people
from that huge amount of suffering and sorrow.
What remains when the mind is brought to its final end
is **Absolutely Perfect**
Infinite Eternal Awareness-Love-Bliss.
That is what I want for as many people as possible.
That is my state of Being always.
That is my Direct Experience.

That state is not a theory, or an idea,
or a belief, or a concept.
It is a living Reality.
You too can know that living Reality.
It requires a dedication to the goal of Manonasa
during all of your waking hours, every day.
It requires all of your heart, all of your mind,
and all of your soul.

When M brought someone else with him
to the Krishnamurti Talks
after the talk he did not ignore the person
he brought with him.

Therefore, after the Talk for most of the day
the attention was on the person he brought with him.

Back to the days
when M had not brought anyone else with him,
let's review and continue:
For one hour after the Talk had ended
M reflected on what K just said.
Then M visited the horse.
Then M decided where to go for lunch.
Then M drove to lunch.

When M was driving the car to lunch
all of his attention was on driving that car safely.
In 40 years of driving cars,
M never had an accident or collision
when M was driving the car.
People get into car collisions for many reasons.
One of those reasons is distracted driving.
The driver of the car looks at the person
on the passenger seat for one second
and that one second of not looking at the road
is enough for a car collision or as they say a car accident.

The problem with the word accident
it that it tends to imply something random
that could not have been prevented.
Almost every so called car "accident"
could have been prevented.

There is an important principle.
If a person does something risky
let's say one hundred times,
and that behavior does not lead to
negative consequences
any of those one hundred times, the person
begins to view that behavior as safe.

Then let's say on the 173rd time
the person does that same behavior,
the behavior causes a car collision
and everyone in the car
and maybe people who were in other cars
are now dead, or alive and paralyzed for life,
or in chronic pain for the rest of their life.

This principle of being fooled into thinking
a risky behavior is a safe behavior
because one has repeated the behavior many times
without negative consequences
applies not only to driving a car.
There are hundreds or thousands of such behaviors.
Skiing down a mountain for example.

Back to the example of driving a car,
here are some more behaviors
where because a person has done the behavior
for more than one hundred times
without negative consequences,
they are fooled into thinking
they are engaging in a safe behavior:

1. The driver picking up something
sitting on the passenger seat or anywhere in the car
where the driver reaches for something.

2. The driver eating in the car.
For example looking down for one second
to pick up that French fry.
Or not looking down, but just being distracted
because eating in the car causes divided attention.

3. The driver talking on a cell phone
while driving.

4. The driver looking away from the road
at people, places or things that are not on the road.
For example a billboard, or a cow.

5. The driver driving a car
after having consumed alcohol.

6. The driver driving a car
while being under the influence of some other substance
that can impair driving ability.

7. The driver driving a car
when they have not had enough sleep.

8. The driver going faster than the speed limit.

9. The driver thinking about something
other than driving the car.

The solution is never do any of that.
While driving a car:
Never look away from the road
not even for a second.
Never eat in the car.
Never talk on a cell phone.
Never drive a car after you have consumed alcohol
regardless of the quantity of alcohol.
If you have had one drop of beer or wine
or some other alcoholic beverage, never drive a car.
Think about driving the car while driving the car,
do not think about other things.

All of this comes down to understanding this
principle of how when one has engaged in a behavior
many times without negative consequences
one stops seeing that the behavior is risky or dangerous
and an unnecessary risk.

To continue with the J. Krishnamurti story,
on a day when M had not brought anyone else with him
to the Krishnamurti Talks, etc.:
M reflected upon what K had just said
for one hour after the Talk was over.
M paid attention only to the horse
while visiting the horse.
M paid attention only to driving
while driving the car to lunch.

So what happened at lunch?
M paid attention only to lunch.
M is looking at the menu to see
how many vegetarian foods they have.
M is wondering on this Menu
are there any vegetarian foods that are:
oh so yummy, yummy, yummy
for the tummy, tummy, tummy.

Paying attention to each step,
ordering the food in a nice tone of voice
when talking to the waiter,
saying thank you when the food is brought.
Paying attention to the food while eating it
and not thinking about other things.

One more thing about lunch.
Often after the Krishnamurti Talk ended
there was an option of having food
right there on the Krishnamurti Foundation property,
maybe five minutes walking from the Oak Grove.
Not cooked food but things like vegetarian sandwiches
and beverages.

Sometimes
if M had brought someone else with him to the Talks
M and the other person would go and eat
one of those sandwiches.

Whole wheat bread, sprouts, avocado,
some great tasting vegetarian dressing, etc.
Those sandwiches were:
oh so yummy, yummy, yummy
for the tummy, tummy, tummy.

When M did not bring anyone with him
to the Talks they were no longer serving food
by the time M finished reflecting
on what K had said in the Oak Grove.

Therefore the price of that reflection
was to miss those sandwiches
that were, need I remind you?:
oh so yummy, yummy, yummy
for the tummy, tummy, tummy.

Almost all humans get fooled by the mind.
The mind tells them "Oh no, you don't want to miss those yummy sandwiches."
People listen to that mind and follow that mind.

One of the keys to the lessons
on what has been written here so far
about M attending Krishnamurti's Talks
is what Krishnamurti once said to a crowd:

"**Have you really listened?
No you have not listened,
because if you had really listened
you would have left here with
ecstatic mind**."

Whatever the various different reasons
people chose not to stay and reflect on what K had said
immediately after the Talk had ended,
while the Talk was still fresh in mind,
they were missing an opportunity
to leave with Ecstatic Mind.

Given a choice between Eternal Ecstasy
and a yummy sandwich
do you think most humans would choose
the yummy sandwich
or do you think most humans would choose
Eternal Ecstasy?

The answer is almost all humans
would choose the yummy sandwich.
Almost all spiritual seekers would choose
the yummy sandwich instead of Eternal Ecstasy.

The reason for that is because
humans are controlled by the ego illusion.
The ego illusion knows that Eternal Ecstasy
is only possible when the ego illusion
comes to its final end.
Therefore the ego illusion controls thinking, beliefs,
concepts, ideas, actions, feelings and desires
**to make sure that spiritual seekers
continually make the choices
that will lead to the ego illusion continuing.**
Almost all humans including spiritual seekers
spend their whole lives trying to avoid Eternal Ecstasy.

The false self, thinking, thoughts, concepts,
beliefs, etc. are thousands of layers of self-deception
and preferring a yummy sandwich
to Eternal Ecstasy is an example of that.
Or preferring anything to Eternal Ecstasy
is an example of that.

To continue the story of M
on a day when he attended Krishnamurti's Talks, etc.
without bringing anyone with him:

After lunch M would go back to the Motel
there in Ojai, California.
What would M do in the motel room?
Sometimes he would continue to ask the question
"What did K say in his Talk today?"

However, more often than not
M would read one of Krishnamurti's books
or one of the Krishnamurti recordings
he had brought with him from Las Vegas.
It is better to ask the question
"What did K say in his Talk today?"
while the Talk is still fresh in the memory.

In that motel room on a little end table
next to the bed there was a book.
The title of the book is *The Teaching of Buddha.*

M knew that for the two week period
he would be in Ojai for the purpose of
attending Krishnamurti's Talks, etc.
that it would be better to stay focused
only on Krishnamurti's teachings
and not any other teachings.
That is because it is a trick of the mind
to always be dividing the attention,
going from one teaching to another so fast
that one never really focuses on a single teaching.
By "trick of the mind" is meant
an ego preservation strategy.
A strategy or trick the ego uses to preserve
and continue its imaginary self.

From body age 15 until around body age 40
M read more than two thousand spiritual books from
almost all of the different spiritual and religious paths.
This was a mistake that M kept making
over and over again for around 25 years.

M's mind told him that the reason
he was reading all those books is because of
the desire for Truth and Freedom from the ego.
However, the real reasons M was reading those books
was because of a fear that if he was not familiar
with all known spiritual paths
how could he know he was on the best
and most effective path?

The other reason M read all those books
is an ego preservation strategy.
It is practice and not books
that brings the ego mind to its final end.
Reading a small number of the most Direct Teachings
can be a big help just like a very clear map
and a very good travel guide can be a big help.

However, reading two thousand books
is not a big help just as reading two thousand maps
will not help you to find the most direct route
from point A to point B.
A small number of clearly written maps
and a small number of clearly written travel guides
is very helpful for finding
the most direct route from point A to point B.

The motel owner or management
had placed a copy of that book
The Teaching of Buddha in every room.
M had never read that particular book before.
Seeing that Buddha book there was very tempting.

Take for example chocolates
and someone who is trying not to eat
any more chocolates even though
they really like eating chocolates.
The person might have enough discipline
not to go to the store and buy chocolates
because they really want to stop that habit
of eating chocolates.
However, let us suppose the Motel
has put a complimentary box of chocolates
on the end table right next to the bed.
The person is lying in bed
and the person does not even have to get out of bed
to reach for that box of chocolates.

That person can grab that box of chocolates
from that end table while lying in bed.
In one second that person
who loves chocolates can grab that box.
When a person loves eating chocolate
and there is a box of chocolates within reach
right next to the bed
it is almost as though that person can hear
that box of chocolates say
"eat me, eat me, eat me, eat me, eat me."

This Motel did not provide a box of chocolates.
This Motel provided a copy of the book
The Teaching of Buddha
and put that book within reach of the bed.

M almost always preferred to read in bed.
Somehow reading in bed
helped to completely forget the body
and concentrate totally on what was being read.

M is laying in bed
and has a Krishnamurti book in his hand.
M had such a strong desire to read that book
The Teaching of Buddha
it was almost as if that book was saying
"read me, read me, read me, read me."

All M had to do is reach
and in one second without even having to get out of bed
he would have that Buddha book in his hand.

So are you wondering what did M do?
M put that Krishnamurti book down
and grabbed *The Teaching of Buddha* book
and spent way too much time reading it.

The point is not that Krishnamurti's teaching
is better than that Buddhist teaching.
The point is also not that that Buddhist teaching
is better than Krishnamurti's teaching.

The point is that it is an ego trick
to keep going from one teaching to another.
The point is to focus on one teaching at a time
so that the one teaching has a chance to penetrate
those thousands of layers of self deception
called the human mind.

M had a very strong desire for Self Realization
from body age 15 onward.
Usually M exhibited behavior
that represented an uncompromising iron will
in the direction of making sure every action
was contributing to Self Realization.

However, when it came to books,
M kept making the same mistake over and over again.
Thousands of times he kept making the same mistake.
That is how more than two thousand spiritual books
were read.

What finally allowed M to see
that reading so many spiritual books is a mistake
is the very, very, very strong desire
for the Freedom of Self Realization
that M had when his body was in its teens,
and twenty's and thirty's
eventually turned into a desire for Self Realization
that was ten million times stronger
than the desire for Self Realization that M had
when his body was in its teens, twenty's, and thirty's.

The desire for Self Realization
that M had when his body was in its teens, twenty's
and thirty's was so very strong
that not even one in ten million humans
has a desire for Self Realization that is that strong.

The more you know about M's actions at that time
the more you can see that his whole life was centered
around Self Realization.
M dropped almost everything out of his life
that had nothing to do with Self Realization.

Now just imagine what it is like
for that very strong desire for Self Realization
to become ten million times stronger than it was.

When the desire for Self Realization
became ten million times stronger
it had as much energy as the Sun.

Just think of how much energy the Sun has.
Almost every plant on earth owes its life
to the energy of the Sun.

The animal kingdom,
which includes human bodies,
all owe their life to the energy of the Sun
for many reasons.

When the desire for Self Realization
became ten million times stronger than it was,
the lack of self honesty that would allow M
to read more than two thousand spiritual books
even though that reading
can never produce Self Realization,
was no longer possible.

Although the self honesty
had been quite extraordinary before,
now the Self honesty was also
ten million times stronger.

Even when M's body was in its teens
M had read quotes by Ramana Maharshi
warning about how a scholar has all those books
as an impediment, etc.

However,
the ego-mind can block out and not dwell on anything
it wants to block out and not dwell on.

The first step in the book
The Seven Steps to Awakening is a collection of quotes
about the fact that an intellectual journey
is not a journey to Self Realization.
Almost every human who thinks they are moving
towards Self Realization
are actually only on an intellectual journey
that is not moving towards Self Realization.

Given a choice between watching television
and reading spiritual books,
M would prefer to read spiritual books.
Reading spiritual books is definitely
a better choice than watching television.

There were two mistakes that M made
for around 25 years:

1. Reading too many spiritual books
instead of using that time for practicing
so that M's amount of time spent practicing every day
was less than the amount of time M spent reading.

2. When M was very, very, very tired
M would prefer to watch television instead of either reading spiritual books or doing spiritual practice.

The lack of self honesty that would allow those two mistakes to be made disappeared when the extremely intense desire for liberation became ten million times stronger and had as much energy as the sun.

Books can be very helpful for attaining Manonasa or in other words Self Realization.
However, they must be the right books,
a small number of Direct Path books
where the communication is Clear and Direct
and the book is written
by one who has attained Manonasa
and the reflections of
the foolish thoughts of the questioner
are not a part of the book.
Not books which simply have the reputation for being Direct Path books.

This is a Ramana Maharshi quote
from the book *The Importance of Practice & Effort*:

Questioner: "Is intellectual knowledge enough?"

Maharshi: "Unless intellectually known,
how to practice it?
Learn it intellectually first,
then do not stop with that.
Practice it."

Yes a small number of the right books
can be very, very, very, very, helpful.

Eventually that desire for Manonasa
that had become ten million times stronger
became trillions of times stronger.
The desire for Manonasa
that had as much energy as the sun
now had as much energy as a trillion stars.

Most people are not very familiar with
big numbers like a million, a billion, a trillion, etc.
So in order to understand what I am trying to convey
here I will tell you a few things about those big numbers.

I have heard that people
in some parts of the world use the word billion
differently than it is used in the USA.
What I will be pointing out here
is the way these words are used in the USA.

One thousand times one thousand is a million.
This is one million: 1,000,000.

One thousand million is a billion:
1,000,000,000.

One thousand billion is a trillion:
1,000,000,000,000.

Since it is almost impossible
to conceive of a trillion
if we look at what a staggering number a billion is
and then remember that you have to have 1000
of those billions to make a trillion
you can get some sense of what a trillion is.

You know how short a time one minute is.
One billion minutes = 1,900 years.
Yes that is right, one thousand nine hundred years.

A little more than one billion minutes ago
Christ was walking the earth.

The Sun is a star.
Think about how much energy the sun has.
Now multiply that times a trillion.
M's desire for Manonasa eventually had as much energy
and intensity as a trillion stars.

Nisargadatta Maharaj said:

"You must be extreme to reach the Supreme."

The reason you have to be extreme
to reach the Supreme
and the reason Manonasa is so rare
that less than one in every five hundred million humans
attains Manonasa is because:

The human mind is made of
thousands of layers of self deception.
Thoughts, ideas, concepts, feelings, desires and beliefs
are being controlled by that ego-mind.
That ego-mind wants to continue.
That ego-mind does not want Manonasa.
That ego-mind has millions of tricks that it can use
to make sure that Manonasa never happens.
That ego-mind has as many tricks and deceptions to
draw upon as there are possible different combinations
of thoughts, ideas, beliefs, concepts, feelings, desires.

It is possible for the ego-mind
to realize the need for its own end.
However it is very rare for that to happen,
because all those tricks
are trying to prevent seeing the need for its own end.

It is very rare for
the desire of the ego-mind to end
to be greater than the ego-mind's desire to continue.
However, it can and does sometimes happen.

FIRST TRIP TO INDIA

In February of 1986 M made his first trip to India.
M went to India with the mother of his body
and her husband at that time
(she has had many husbands).
The mother made the travel arrangements.
Instead of flying directly from Singapore to India
the group of three flew from Singapore to Sri Lanka.
The group spent three days in Sri Lanka.

In Sri Lanka the group
went to a place called The Temple of the Tooth.
It supposedly has one of the Buddha's teeth.

There was a place in Sri Lanka where the group
could watch an elephant being bathed in a river.
The elephant was laying down in the river
with its trunk up in the air so that it could breathe.
The person would use the coconut shell as a bowl
and pour water on the area of the elephant
they were going to scrub next
then scrub the elephant's skin with the coconut shell.

M asked the people if he could scrub the elephant.
They said yes, so M took off his shoes and socks,
went in the water,
used the coconut shell as a bowl to pour some water
on a portion of the elephant's skin
and used the coconut shell to scrub the elephant.

The coconut shell was hard
and M was a little bit concerned
that the scrubbing might hurt the elephant.
However, M thought that the elephant handlers
knew what they are doing and therefore of course
this would not hurt the elephant.
Also putting water on the coconut
probably made the shell not quite as hard.
The people laughed at M scrubbing the elephant
because tourists normally just watch other people
scrubbing the elephant.
Tourists do not normally ask
if they can scrub the elephant.

Most humans are like spiritual tourists.
People will read, discuss, say "isn't it interesting
that Ramana Maharshi attained Manonasa"
**but they will not do what has to be done
so that they too can attain Manonasa**.

Those spiritual tourists,
which includes almost every spiritual seeker
who has ever lived in the history of mankind
are like those tourists
who watch someone else scrub an elephant
and think they now know what
the experience of scrubbing an elephant is like.

If you want to know
what the experience of scrubbing an elephant is like
you have to take your socks and shoes off
and go into the water
and then use the coconut shell as a bowl
to pour some water on the elephant's skin
and then you have to scrub the elephant's skin
with the coconut shell.

If you want to be one of those extremely rare,
less than one out of five hundred million humans
who attains Manonasa
you have to drop all of your unnecessary activities
and devote all of the free time thus created
to practicing the most direct means to Manonasa.

There was a place in Sri Lanka
where people could ride an elephant.
The other two people in the group of three
declined that opportunity.
M said yes he wants to ride the elephant.
M bought a bunch of bananas
that M planned on feeding to the elephant
after the ride was over.
While M was riding the elephant,
the elephant put its own trunk over its own head
towards the bananas that M was holding.
So M, one by one fed the bananas to the elephant
while M was riding the elephant.
M did not know that an elephant
could put its own trunk all the way over its own head
so far that it could reach the person riding the elephant.
You can imagine how surprised M was to see that trunk
coming towards his body.
It is a funny image.
By putting its trunk over its own head towards M
while M was riding the elephant,
the elephant was communicating (through that action):
"Yes I know you have bananas.
I have a method of grabbing those bananas
while you are up there riding."

On February 17, 1986 the group of three
flew from Sri Lanka to Madras India.
The name of the city of Madras
has been officially changed to Chennai.
However, back in 1986 it was still called Madras.
Many people still use the old name Madras even today.

M decided to stay in a different hotel
than the other two members of the group.
The hotel had a big fancy name,
maybe it was called Madras International Hotel.
However, it was a very small hotel that was not fancy.

In India many hotels,
including many very small hotels,
slide a newspaper under the door in the morning.
There is a small gap between
the bottom of the room door and the floor.
On the morning of February 18, 1986
M was surprised to see that newspaper
because this was his first trip to India.

Before reading that newspaper
M had called the front desk
to request that a person be sent to the room
to fix some maintenance problem.

M began reading the newspaper.
The newspaper stated that
J. Krishnamurti had passed away.
M began crying.
The maintenance person arrived
and went about fixing the maintenance problem.

M was crying the whole time
the maintenance person was there.
M kept his face hidden behind the newspaper
because he did not want the maintenance person
to see him crying.
However,
M had been crying when he answered the door
and showed the maintenance person
the maintenance problem
and therefore the maintenance person knew
that M was crying.

After fixing the maintenance problem
the maintenance person left the room.
Later there was a knock at the door.
It was a woman who managed the hotel.
The maintenance person had told her that M was crying
and she was there to find out why M was crying.
M told her the reason he was crying
was because the newspaper had stated that
J. Krishnamurti has died.
The manager asked M did you know Krishnamurti?
M said I did not know him personally
but I had attended his Talks in two previous years
and I have tickets to attend his talks
that were scheduled for this spring.
I was planning on attending his talks again
after I return to America.

M was not aware that he had
such deep feelings for J. Krishnamurti
until he read that newspaper article and started crying.
M knew that he liked J. Krishnamurti,
but he did not know he had those deep feelings
for Krishnamurti until he read that newspaper.

The group of three went to Bangalore.
The reason for going to Bangalore is
it was a place to spend a night or two
before going to Satya Sai Baba's ashram.

The group of three stayed in a place called
the Woodlands Hotel.
This was a small hotel
and it definitely was not a fancy hotel.
Or in other words it was not modern.

M had never seen a toilet like the one in the room.
The water tank was up high on the wall.
M pulled the chain or cord once.
Nothing happened.
It took M a long time to figure out
that you have to pull the cord many times very fast
over and over and over to get it to flush.

The group of three took a taxi
from Bangalore to Satya Sai Baba's ashram.
The name of the taxi service was Om Sai Ram.
Sai Baba's Ashram is called Prasanthi Nilayam
(Abode of Supreme Peace).

Satya Sai Baba's body was still living in 1986
therefore they were able to see Satya Sai Baba.

There is going to be a very valuable lesson
described here in the story of the visit to Satya Sai Baba,
however,
let's get a humorous incident out of the way first:
Even the western woman who had never worn a Sari
before in their lives wore Sari's at Sai Baba's ashram.
Therefore, the mother of M's body bought a Sari.
The funny thing is
she could not figure out how to wear it, how to put it on.

At one point M and the mother's husband held the Sari
while the mother wound herself round and round
trying to get the Sari to wrap around her.
Of course that did not work either.
If you can picture them holding that Sari
while she twists round and round
that is a very funny image!

Now begins the very powerful lesson.
If you put this lesson into practice,
this lesson can change your life
and help your spiritual progress greatly.

Around ten years previously,
maybe in 1976 give or take a year,
M had read in a very popular Satya Sai Baba book
the following quote by Sai Baba:
"I have come to give you the key
to the treasure of Ananda (Bliss)
to teach you how to tap that spring,
for you have forgotten the way to blessedness.
If you waste this time of saving yourselves,
it is just your fate.
You have come to get from me tinsel and trash,
the petty little cures and promotions,
worldly joys and comforts.
Very few of you desire to get from me
the thing I have come to give you:
namely, liberation itself.
Even among these few,
those who stick to the path of Sadhana
(spiritual practice), and succeed are a handful."

If someone is suffering from some terrible disease
and Satya Sai Baba cures them of that disease
it may be hard for them to understand
how that can be a "petty little cure" or "tinsel and trash"
however, compared to Eternal Bliss
and Eternal Liberation,
all that is temporary is just tinsel and trash and is petty.
Being cured of a physical ailment
will not solve the problem of suffering.
You will still be reborn for
8,000,000,000,000,000,000,000,000
imaginary lifetimes
and during those lifetimes
you will over and over and over again
die of all of the thousands of diseases
that a human body is prone to.
One lifetime it will be one disease
another lifetime it will be another disease.
During that huge number of future imaginary lifetimes
you will over and over experience
every possible type of horror and suffering and sorrow.
When the word imaginary is used,
remember this lifetime is also imaginary.
All of those lifetimes will seem as real
as this lifetime does to you now.
During that huge number of future imaginary lifetimes
you will experience the equivalent of
4,000,000,000,000,000 oceans of suffering
and sorrow.

The Eternal Bliss of Liberation
puts an end to all of that suffering and sorrow
for all of eternity.
Being cured of one disease in one lifetime is indeed
a petty little cure compared to being cured of
the ego-mind parasite which will end all rebirths
and therefore all diseases for all of eternity.

Thus if you remind yourself of
what was written on the previous page
and the fact that only the Eternal Bliss of Liberation
can put an end to all that sorrow and suffering,
that will help you to be motivated to attain Manonasa,
which is the same as Nirvana and Self-Realization,
and to do what it takes to attain Manonasa.

All of the thousands of types of miracles
that Satya Sai Baba performed were
temporary phenomena that can never liberate anyone.
Because they are temporary
and because they can never liberate anyone
they are indeed as Satya Sai Baba stated it:
"tinsel and trash" "petty."

M remembered that quote he had read
by Satya Sai Baba around ten years previously.
While M was there at Satya Sai Baba's ashram
most of the time M had his eyes closed.
The reason M had his eyes closed
is because Liberation and Eternal Bliss are within,
they are not in the realm of that which can be seen
with physical eyes.

When Satya Sai Baba
came walking past M's body,
M did not see Satya Sai Baba
because M had his eyes closed.
M was one of those one in a million seekers
who did not come for tinsel and trash!
M came for Liberation!

Many seekers lie to themselves
and also think they have come for Liberation.
Their behavior and their actions prove
they are not really trying to be Liberated at all!

One day the husband of M's mother
tapped M on the shoulder
because he did not want M to miss
the materialization of Vibhuti (ash) that Satya Sai Baba
was doing for the person seated next to M.
Therefore, M opened his eyes
and saw the Vibhuti forming in Satya Sai Baba's hand
and saw the Vibhuti falling into the person's hand.
Satya Sai Baba was only standing one foot
from M's body therefore M could see the Vibhuti
forming in Satya Sai Baba's hand very clearly.
It was a huge amount of Vibhuti
that Satya Sai Baba poured into the person's hand.
Maybe ¼ cup.

If the mother's husband
had not tapped M on the shoulder
M would have never at any time
during the trip to Satya Sai Baba's ashram
seen one of the miraculous phenomena
that Sai Baba was performing
because M kept his eyes closed.
Why did M keep his eyes closed?
Because M was not there for petty tinsel and trash!
M was there because he wanted the Eternal Bliss
that can only come from Liberation
and M did not want anything else!

When M opened his eyes
to see the materialization
he noticed everyone in the crowd had their eyes open.
Every time M opened his eyes
because it was time to get up and leave
he noticed everyone in the crowd had their eyes open.

It is **not** because of grace, magic, fate, destiny or luck that M eventually became one of those less than one in five hundred million humans who attain Manonasa. M's approach, M's actions, were completely different from the crowd. That is why M eventually attained Manonasa.

Reflect upon this quote by Lao Tzu from the Hua Hu Ching:

"**Not all spiritual paths**
lead to the Harmonious Oneness.
Indeed, most are distractions and detours,
nothing more."

If your ego-mind will allow the meaning of that quote to penetrate through those thousands of layers of self deception so that you can really see the meaning it can completely change your view of the spiritual teachings of the past.

M was the member of a number of online spiritual groups. When he posted that Lao Tzu quote there was a very predictable reaction. People would write something like this: *even though the spiritual paths may be distractions and detours, maybe they are necessary steps at a particular stage of a person's spiritual development.* If you wanted a very specific example of how those thousands of layers of self deception distort what is read to change something that was intended to help bring the ego-mind to an end into something that will preserve the ego-mind, people's reaction to the Lao Tzu quote in *italics* above is that very specific example.

It is as though Lao Tzu knew exactly
how the ego-mind was going to distort
what he was saying.
That is why Lao Tzu added the words
Nothing More!

If those spiritual paths were necessary steps
for a particular stage of a person's spiritual development
then they would be something more
than a distraction or detour!
If they were necessary steps
for a particular stage in a person's spiritual development
then they would be leading a person to the
Harmonious Oneness
by taking care of that necessary step.
He said they do **not** lead to the Harmonious Oneness.
He said **nothing more**.
LOOK! LOOK! LOOK! LOOK!
SEE HOW THE HUMAN MIND
REFUSES TO SEE
THE MEANING OF LAO TZU'S QUOTE.
SEE HOW THE HUMAN MIND CHANGES
LAO TZU'S QUOTE
INTO SOMETHING COMPLETELY DIFFERENT!
SOMETHING THAT WILL JUSTIFY
THE SPIRITUAL TEACHINGS OF THE PAST
WHICH DO **NOT** LEAD TO
THE HARMONIOUS ONENESS

AND WHICH ARE:

DISTRACTIONS AND DETOURS,
NOTHING MORE!

Nothing More!
Nothing More!
Nothing More!

Humans believe their thoughts, concepts, ideas, opinions, beliefs, etc.
From the time a human wakes up in the morning
until they go to sleep at night
a human's thoughts, concepts, ideas, opinions, beliefs, etc. are being directed by the ego-mind
to preserve and continue the ego-mind.
The ego-mind selects a false spiritual teaching
that will help the ego-mind to continue.
And almost all spiritual teachings are false
spiritual teachings aimed at preserving the ego-mind
including almost all of those teachings
that claim to be for the purpose of ending the ego-mind.

Most spiritual teachings were created
by those still under the illusion of the ego.
All of those spiritual teachings
are for the purpose of preserving the ego-illusion
even if they state they are for the purpose
of bringing the ego-illusion to an end.

Some of the spiritual teachings of the past
were created by someone who had attained Manonasa.
From the very first time the ego-mind hears or reads
such a teaching,
it changes the teaching into something
that will preserve the ego-mind
instead of something that will end the ego-mind.

After a spiritual teaching
that was created by one who has attained Manonasa
has been distorted by the ego,
and that happens instantly,
from that moment on
the spiritual teaching serves to preserve the ego-illusion
and does **not** help to bring the ego illusion to an end.

Almost **none** of the people in human history that people *believe* attained Manonasa, Nirvana, Jivan-mukti, Self Realization, Union with the Infinite, Union with the Divine, Union with the Supreme Being etc. actually attained those goals.
Thinking or believing that someone
who has **not** attained Manonasa, Nirvana, etc.
has attained Manonasa, Nirvana, etc.
is an ego preservation strategy.
It contributes to the false belief that the spiritual teachings of the past actually succeed in their goal.
They do not succeed in their goal.
Thinking that someone
who really **has** attained Manonasa, Nirvana, etc.
has **not** attained Manonasa, Nirvana, etc.
is also an ego preservation strategy.
It makes the ego avoid the teaching
of the one who really has attained Manonasa, etc.

There have been more than 15,000 wars
in the last five thousand years.
Every day there are billions of acts of violence
that are not a part of war.
Billions of people hurt each other verbally
or physically every day.
All of the verbal and physical violence
and all of the other ways humans hurt each other
and hurt animals comes from the ego-mind.
The ego-mind is evil.

Because all of the spiritual teachings
of the past are helping to preserve the ego-illusion,
all of the spiritual teachings of the past are evil.

All humans lie to themselves
from the time they wake up in the morning
until they go to sleep at night.

If you are wondering
what the solution to all this is,
the solution is to awaken
the extremely intense desire for Manonasa
which is the same as Nirvana and Self realization.
There are some suggestions in the book
The Direct Means to Eternal Bliss as to how to
Awaken the Extremely intense desire for Manonasa
such as facing the entire ocean of human evil,
sorrow and suffering.
Reading the Step Five quotes in the book
The Seven Steps to Awakening
is a positive way to increase the desire for Manonasa.
You can try those suggestions if you wish.
However,
you should not limit yourself to just those suggestions.
You should find out what will increase
your desire for Manonasa to an extremely intense level.
You should experiment and find out
what increases your desire for Manonasa
to an extremely intense level.

Almost everything in this book
is going to cause an ego reaction in most people.
This book has not been published yet
as I am writing this.
Therefore, no reviews have been written
of the book you are now reading.
When this book is published there are going to be
a huge number of negative reviews.
I know that because the ego reaction is predictable.
In the previous editions of the Eternal Bliss book
there were many negative reviews.
In most of those negative reviews,
there was at least one thing that the reviewer was
criticizing that came from the reviewer's imagination
that was not in the book.

In other words the reviewer would first imagine
something was in the book that was not in the book,
and then criticize the book for that thing
that the reviewer had imagined was in the book
that was not in the book.
The ego was so intent on having a negative reaction
against a book that **truly** challenges the ego,
not like those books that are **pretending**
to challenge the ego but are really supporting the ego,
the reviewer imagined something was in the book
that was not in the book
and then criticized the book
for what they had imagined was in the book.
The negative reviews were not a surprise
for the Eternal Bliss book.
Just as I know that the book you are now reading is
going to cause a reaction by the ego that will produce
negative reviews even though the book has not been
published yet and therefore there are no reviews,
I knew before the first edition of the Eternal Bliss book
was published that it was going to cause
most people to have an ego reaction
and that the ego as a defense strategy
was going to write negative reviews.
What was a surprise were all the positive 5 star reviews.
I did not think the ego would allow so many people
to see the value in the book.
Only a small percentage of people write reviews.
Therefore for every ten people who write a negative
review, there are probably more than
one hundred people who had a negative reaction.

The book you are now reading
was written for that one out of a million spiritual seeker
in whom the desire to end the ego-illusion
is greater than the desire to preserve the ego illusion.

They will not be detoured by
the negative reviews that are coming.
They will love the Truth this book reveals.
They will recognize the Truth this book reveals.

Those one out of a million spiritual seekers
in whom the desire to bring the ego illusion to an end
is greater than the desire to preserve the ego illusion
will love this book.
For those extremely rare ones
this book will be like a breath of fresh air.

The crowd chooses to continue the ego illusion.
The crowd will have
8,000,000,000,000,000,000,000,000
imaginary lifetimes ahead of them
and in those lifetimes
the crowd will experience the equivalent of
4,000,000,000,000,000
oceans of suffering and sorrow.

The crowd will turn towards
one of the spiritual teachings of the past
that are distractions and detours, nothing more
and that do not lead to the Harmonious Oneness.
The crowd will meet together in groups
to help each other preserve the ego illusion.
The crowd will have discussions with each other
to help each other preserve the ego-illusion
while pretending to themselves and to each other
that they are helping each other to end the ego illusion.

There are ways you can begin to see
what the crowd does not see.
Here are four ways
you can open the door to Truth:

1. When you see that one of the spiritual
or religious teachings from the past
that you thought was leading to Truth
is not leading to Truth,
you have opened a doorway to Truth.

2. When you see that one of the spiritual
or religious teachings from the past
that you thought was leading towards
the end of the ego illusion
is actually not leading towards
the end of the ego illusion
you have opened a doorway to Truth.

3. When you see that when
people gather together
either in person or online
to discuss a spiritual or religious teaching
that their real purpose is
to preserve the ego illusion
and not to go towards Truth,
you have opened a doorway to Truth.

4. When you observe your thoughts, feelings, desires,
beliefs, concepts, actions, etc.
from the time you wake up in the morning
until the time you go to sleep at night
and you catch the ego-mind lying to you
and you catch the ego-mind leading you to
spend time engaged in unnecessary activities
that can never lead you towards Awakening,
you have opened a doorway to Truth.

The most successful method
for attaining Manonasa in the history of mankind
has been **a particular type of** Self Awareness Practice.
However, there are still less than one out of every five
hundred million humans who are attaining Manonasa.
Therefore none of those who have attained Manonasa
in the past have been very successful
in helping many humans attain Manonasa.
I am constantly experimenting with better approaches.
I am staying with the most successful method
which is a certain type of Self Awareness practice.

However,
I have made some significant observations
about how to make that practice more successful.
One hour of Self Awareness practice from the Heart
produces more progress towards Manonasa
than one thousand hours of Self Awareness Practice
from the head.
Most people who practice Self Awareness
are usually practicing from their heads
even after many years of practicing Self Awareness.

If people listen to certain spiritual music
before they practice Self Awareness
they can move out of their head
and closer to their Heart.
I have created four spiritual music youtube playlists
for the purpose of helping people move out of their head
and closer to their Heart.
If you go to www.seeseer.com
and then click the "Free" tab
and then click the Self Awareness Practice Instructions
playlist link and then watch the video titled
Self Awareness and the Heart
you can see how to find those spiritual music youtube
playlists and instructions on how to use them.

I have created many videos
and many youtube playlists.
All of the videos are free to watch.
No money changes hands.

The other link on the "Free" page
is to the Eternal Bliss Yahoo Group.
It is a newsletter type group
which means only the founder posts messages there.
I post quotes there.
The Eternal Bliss Group has more than 2000 members.
You can join that group
and receive the messages I post there in your email.
It is completely free of charge
to join the Eternal Bliss Group
and to receive those messages.
No money changes hands.

There is something very important
that you should know about me:

1. I have never accepted a donation
from one of my spiritual students
and I will never accept a donation
from one of my spiritual students.

2. I have never accepted a donation
from an organization.

The above listed two facts make me different
from almost all spiritual and religious teachers.

What I want from people
is that they achieve Manonasa.
I do not want and I will not accept any donation
from any of my spiritual students.

I will not accept any donations
from any of my spiritual students
because I want them to be sure of
what my motivations are.

In July of 2015
this body had the symptoms of a heart attack.
I had to look the symptoms up online
because this body had never had a heart attack before.
Two of the symptoms matched heart attack symptoms
perfectly.

I did not call an ambulance
because I cannot afford an ambulance
and I also cannot afford the medical care.
I could have asked my students
to each donate what they can afford to donate
so that I could afford medical care, etc.
I did not ask any of my students to donate anything.
I did not tell my students about the heart attack
until three months later.
If any of my students had offered to donate money
to me even without my asking, I would have said **no**.

The body survived.
However, I would have let the body die
before I would have accepted a donation
from one my spiritual students.

The reason for that is as follows.
People are going to be studying and practicing
the books I wrote:

1. *The Direct Means to Eternal Bliss.*
2. *How to Practice the Teachings.*
3. *Manonasa: A Spiritual Autobiography.*

and the books I created
where I carefully selected other teacher's quotes,
and created a **new unique** teaching
by only selecting quotes
that have no distractions and detours
and that do not include a reflection of
the foolish thoughts of the questioner:

4. *The Seven Steps to Awakening.*
5. *Experience Your Perfect Soul.*
6. *The True Self.*
7. *The Importance of Practice & Effort.*
8. *How to Live a Life that Knows Only Love.*

for thousands of years.

It is essential that both those
very rare one in a million seekers today
and those very rare one in a million seekers
that will be reading those books
for hundreds of generations to come in the future
know what my motivations are.
By refusing to ever accept a donation
from any of my students they will be able to see that
I am 100% authentic.
Seeing that I am 100% authentic
will help them to see that
the teachings are 100% authentic.

I want to save as many people as possible
from going through those
8,000,000,000,000,000,000,000,000
imaginary lifetimes
and the 4,000,000,000,000,000
oceans of sorrow and suffering
that people will experience
in those future imaginary lifetimes.

Therefore, if the heart attack
had ended the body life that would have been OK
because all those future generations would know
that I was willing to let the body die
instead of accepting a donation
from any of my spiritual students
just so they would know that
the teachings are 100% authentic.

I will write a Ramana Maharshi quote here.
If your ego-mind allows you to see the meaning
and the quote's many implications,
it will completely revolutionize
and change your view of spiritual teachings,
including
the spiritual teachings of the direct path Sages.

This Ramana Maharshi quote is quote #34
from the book *The Seven Steps to Awakening*:

"The Sage's pure mind
which beholds as a mere witness
the whole world
is like a mirror which
reflects the foolish thoughts
of those who come before him.
And these thoughts
are then *mistaken to be his*."

Almost all spiritual seekers think
that if a Sage says something on a spiritual topic
that what the Sage said
is a part of his or her spiritual teachings.
The above Ramana Maharshi quote
completely destroys that myth.
And that changes everything.

Let us suppose for example that you find a book
that has teachings by one of the seven Sages
quoted in the book *The Seven Steps to Awakening.*
Let us suppose that book is around 700 pages.
That would be a very large book.
Most seekers would assume that everything written
in that book that is on a spiritual topic
is a part of the Sage's teachings
just because the Sage said it.
Quote 34 destroys that idea completely.

Let us suppose in that 700 page book
that 600 pages are quotes by a Sage
when the Sage was only reflecting
the foolish thoughts of those who came before him
and therefore even though the Sage said it,
it is not a part of the Sage's teaching.
Let us suppose that out of that 700 page book
that only 100 pages of what the Sage said
are **not** a reflection of the foolish thoughts
of those who appeared before the Sage.
What do people do? I have had a chance to see what
people do. I have studied the teachings of Ramana
Maharshi, for example, for more than 40 years.
Most of the time when people quote Ramana Maharshi
they are quoting what was
the reflection of the foolish thoughts of the questioner
and even though Ramana Maharshi did say it,
it is **not** a part of Ramana Maharshi's teachings.

The ego does this as a preservation strategy
because the ego knows that
the reflection of the foolish thoughts of the questioner
is not a threat to the ego.

In *The Seven Steps to Awakening*
seven Sages are quoted.
I carefully selected those quotes
and I did **not** include any quotes that were
the reflection of the foolish thoughts of those
who appeared before the Sages.
Therefore *The Seven Steps to Awakening*
is a **unique** book that is a **new** spiritual path.

Prior to the awakening of
the extremely intense desire for Freedom,
spiritual seekers focus on the quotes
that are the least threat to the ego
and that will never lead to Manonasa.
Therefore one obstacle for a spiritual seeker
is if they read a book that has a few very powerful quotes
and hundreds of not so powerful quotes
they do not recognize which quotes
are the most powerful quotes
that contain the keys to Manonasa.
That is one of the many beauties of the book
The Seven Steps to Awakening.
I only included the powerful quotes
that are the keys to Manonasa.

Let us suppose
that someone overcomes the first obstacle
and does recognize a powerful quote
that actually is a key to Manonasa.
Not a quote that the ego-mind that still wishes
to preserve its imaginary self is telling them
is a key to Manonasa.

The next obstacle is that
they usually do not remember the quote.
If they read the quote hundreds of times
that would help.
The awakening of
the extremely intense desire for Manonasa
will help them both to recognize and remember
the key powerful quotes.

The third obstacle the spiritual seeker faces
is that even if he or she does overcome the first obstacle
by recognizing a powerful quote
that is a key to Manonasa
and even if they do remember the quote,
usually they do not apply the quote.
Usually they do not put the quote into practice.

Now let's return to the powerful lessons from the Krishnamurti story and the Satya Sai Baba story.

M recognized a powerful key to Manonasa
that he had heard on a recording by J. Krishnamurti.
Instead of trying to remember hundreds of
Krishnamurti quotes
he just focused on a few powerful quotes
that were keys to Manonasa.

When M heard on a recording
Krishnamurti saying to a crowd:

"**Have you listened?
No you have not listened
because if you had really listened
you would have left here with Ecstatic Mind**."

M recognized that as a very powerful lesson.
M recognized that as a key to Manonasa.

M remembered the quote.
Most people either don't remember a powerful quote or they only remember a powerful quote for a short time.

Years had passed between
when M heard Krishnamurti say that quote
on a recording
and when M first heard Krishnamurti in person.

M had retained that powerful quote in memory.
Then M did what almost no spiritual seeker ever does.
He applied the powerful quote.
He put that powerful quote into action.

It is **not** grace, magic, luck, fate or destiny
that causes a human to be one of the less than one in five hundred million humans who attain Manonasa.
It is the intensity of the desire for Manonasa
that causes a human
to eventually attain Manonasa
because that great desire for Manonasa
makes that human's approach and actions
completely different from the crowd's approach.

When you see a powerful quote write it down
and put it where you will see it every day.

M stayed to reflect on what K had just said
for an hour after everyone else had left.
The key to understanding this is the fact that
M did not allow the mind to go on to some other subject
or some other activity,
but while that Talk was still fresh in mind,
and before the mind had a chance to change the subject
and go onto other actions
M asked "What did K just say?"

Now let's look at the lessons from the Satya Sai Baba story.

Around 1976 M had read a Sai Baba book. He recognized this quote by Sai Baba that is a powerful key to Manonasa:

"I have come to give you the key
to the treasure of Ananda (Bliss),
to teach you how to tap that spring,
for you have forgotten the way to blessedness.
If you waste this time of saving yourselves,
it is just your fate.
You have come to get from me
tinsel and trash,
the petty little cures and promotions,
worldly joys and comforts.
Very few of you desire to get from me the thing
that I have come to give you:
namely, Liberation itself.
Even among those few,
those who stick to the path of Sadhana
(spiritual practice) and succeed
are a handful."

M did not try to remember a huge number of quotes by Sai Baba, he just remembered a few powerful quotes that were keys to Manonasa. Ten years later when M first saw Sai Baba in person, M remembered that powerful quote. And M put that quote into practice. The entire crowd was looking at Sai Baba's phenomena, miracles, materializations, etc. and M had his eyes closed because M was only interested in the Liberation and Bliss that lies within. **M was using a completely different approach than the crowd was using.**

Most people if they remembered a quote
for ten years would remember a quote
that they **believed** to be a powerful key
that in fact is really supporting the ego illusion.
Most people would remember a quote
that although a Sage said it,
was really just a reflection of the foolish thoughts
of those who appeared before the Sage
and therefore **even though the Sage said it,**
it is <u>not</u> a part of the Sage's spiritual teaching.

It is **not** grace, fate, destiny, magic
or some deity that allows those
less than one in five hundred million humans
to attain Manonasa.
It is the extremely intense desire for Manonasa
and the way that desire changes the approach
and the actions
that makes those who eventually attain Manonasa,
attain Manonasa.

Even a powerful quote can be used
by the ego illusion to preserve the ego illusion.
Take for example the part of the Sai Baba quote
where Sai Baba says it is just your fate.

In most people the ego would jump on that
"it is just your fate" part of the quote
and they would say to themselves
there is nothing I can do about any of this because
it is just my fate or destiny.

The book *The Importance of Practice & Effort*
which is a collection of quotes by the Seven Sages
reveals that it is not some deity, grace, fate, destiny, etc.
that leads to Manonasa.
It is practice that leads to Manonasa.

When the group of three were going to leave Sai Baba's ashram the mother of M's body said to Sai Baba we are leaving. Sai Baba told her "Break a coconut."

The next stop for the group of three was
Trivandrum in the state of Kerala
and they saw a priest in a temple there
and paid him a small fee to break a coconut for us
since Sai Baba had said break a coconut.

The group of three went to Kovalum beach next,
also in the state of Kerala.
One surprise for M was that the ocean water was warm.
In San Diego, California beaches
the ocean was always very cold.

One day when M was swimming in the ocean
at Kovalum
he left his eyeglasses on his towel on the beach.
When he returned from swimming
his eyeglasses were gone.
A man approached M
and said that he knew where the eyeglasses were
and that for a fee he would go and get the eyeglasses.
M paid the small fee.

The hotel manager warned M
never to go out at night
because there were bad people there on the beach.
I guess that meant even worse people
than the people who had held his eyeglasses
for ransom.

M observed something interesting
there at Kovalum. A busload of people from some
other part of India would get off the bus and spend
all of their time watching the foreigners on the beach.

M made 6 trips to India
that averaged three months each.
Therefore M spent one and a half years in India.
In all of those trips to India
he noticed that people from India
called people who were not from India "foreigners."

The group of three went to the train station
in Trivandrum.
They were going to take a train ride
to a city called Cochin.
The group of three boarded the train.
M had misread the time on the train ticket
and thought he had plenty of time
to go and get some apple juice.
The mother's husband said to M you had better hurry.
M went to get some apple juice.
The apple juice was a long walk away
at the other end of the train station.

As M was returning to the train
and getting closer to the train
it appeared as though the train was leaving.
Sure enough, yes indeed the train was leaving.
M started running hoping to catch the train.
M's belt broke and M's pants were falling off
as he was running.
The locals were laughing at that.

By the time M got to where the train was
the train was going much too fast
and was too far away for M to catch it.
M had seen so many Hollywood western movies as a
child where people were able to run and catch a train.
Things do not always work out in life
like they do in the movies.

M's passport and traveler's checks
were there on the train
with the mother and her husband.
M only had a small amount of rupees in his pocket.
The question was how would M get to Cochin
and even if he did get to Cochin
how would he find the mother, her husband,
and therefore his passport and travelers checks?
Buses are not expensive in India
and M had enough rupees for a bus to Cochin.
All this was scary for M
because M wondered if he did not find the mother
and the husband
he would not have his passport or travelers checks.
Then what would he do?
Since this was his first trip to India
M was not familiar with India
and India is a very different place from the USA.

The mother and her husband and M
had discussed some hotels located in Cochin
that were mentioned in a travel book.
M had told the other two
which hotel was his preference.
When M arrived in Cochin he decided to go to that hotel
and see if the mother and her husband were there.

The clerk behind the front desk at the hotel
said no they are not registered here.
Then the clerk asked to see M's passport.
M told the clerk that is what I have been telling you
they have my passport.
Somehow that rang a bell with the desk clerk.
The desk clerk showed M the hotel register
and fortunately the mother and the husband
were there at the hotel. Therefore,
M now had his travelers checks and his passport.

The mother and her husband
were only visiting India for a short time.
M had planned a three month trip.
Therefore it was known from the beginning
that M would at some point continue traveling alone
and the mother and her husband
would be returning to America.

With the various things that happened
on the various trips to India
I do not always remember on which trip or on what date
a particular event happened.
Therefore when I don't know which trip or which date
I will just write "On a trip to India"
or something along those lines.

CHAPTER FOUR

WHEN THE BODY WAS IN ITS THIRTY'S

On one of the many trips M made to
Tiruvannamalai (maybe the first trip)
M stayed in a room on the second floor of a hotel.
M noticed outside the window that a monkey
had climbed up a telephone pole
and was very close to the window.
M had an apple and put the apple on a suitcase
on the bed and made sure the monkey saw the apple.
Then M opened the window
and went to the opposite side of the room.
The monkey came in the room very slowly and calmly
and the monkey picked up the apple
and the monkey left the room very slowly and calmly
and went back to the telephone pole.
It was interesting that the monkey knew
the apple had been placed there for him.
The monkey knew it did not need to be in a hurry
or aggressively grab the apple.
The monkey was not interested in any other food
in the room.
The monkey was only there to collect the apple
that had been placed on the suitcase for him.

In that same room the next day
the items M had on a table began to shake.
M went down to tell the people at the front desk
about what had happened.
They said that if M wanted them to send someone
to look at the room to try to figure out what happened
they would do it.

Then, while M was still at the front desk
people began rushing in from the outside
saying there had been an earthquake.
Apparently earthquakes
had been very rare in Tiruvannamalai
because no one could remember
there ever having been an earthquake before.
The next day the newspaper stated
there had been a very strong earthquake and that the
epicenter was in the ocean 50 miles from Pondicherry.

From time to time M would talk to a woman
who was a tailor in Tiruvannamalai.
She was from Kerala
and her native language was Malayalam.
M bought a cassette with Ramana Maharshi Bhajans
in Malayalam at Sri Ramanasramam
and gave it as a gift to the tailor woman.
She was surprised that M remembered
that she was from Kerala
and that her native language was Malayalam.
The gift brought tears to her eyes.
Sometimes it is very easy to do a kind and caring action
even for people one does not know well.

M went to Dal Lake in Srinagar, Kashmir.
M stayed on a houseboat.
Small boats bring all kinds of things
to the big houseboat.
One boat will have bottled water and snacks.
Another will have locally made items.
If you ever stay on a houseboat in Kashmir,
be sure to look for peepholes.
The owners like to drill many tiny peepholes
so that no guest really has any privacy,
not even in the bathroom. You discover the peepholes
at night by the little light shining through them.

One time M went to Ladakh.
Ladakh is in the Himalayas.
The majority of people in Ladakh are Tibetan Buddhists.
Supposedly spring had just begun
but it really seemed like winter.
The roads had not thawed yet
and therefore the only way to get vegetables
was to fly them in.
When someone had vegetables for sale
there would be long lines
and M saw a fight break out in one of those lines.
The two exceptions were carrots and potatoes.
Those were readily available even in winter.
It was funny to see the menu in a local restaurant
that read something like potato and carrot soup,
potato and carrot pie, potatoes and carrots,
spiced potatoes and carrots, fried potatoes and carrots,
steamed potatoes and carrots, potato and carrot bread,
potato and carrot cake, etc., etc, etc.,

The water for the little guest house
had to be brought from a river.
M saw an old lady getting that water.
M offered to carry the water for her.
Due to the elevation, M was having difficulty breathing
due to the strain of trying to carry the water.
Thus the lady felt sorry for M
and decided it was best for her to carry the water.
It did not appear to be a strain for her to carry the water.
There is something funny about the old lady
seeing M huffing and puffing and feeling sorry for him
and deciding she should carry the water.
The guest house was very cold.
M for some strange reason (maybe intuition)
had bought some vegetables in Delhi and put them in
his suitcase. He gave them to the hotel owner who
cooked them and all the guests had vegetables.

M took a train ride from Madras to Patna.
The reason for going to Patna is it is a place to rest
before going to Bod Gaya,
the place of the Buddha's enlightenment.

There was a change of trains in Calcutta.
In Calcutta M was having difficulty finding
the correct window to buy the ticket for Patna.
M had a second class AC Indrail Pass that allowed him
unlimited travel on the trains for 30 days.
Second class AC might sound second class,
however the AC stands for air conditioning
and second class AC was super deluxe and very nice.
M went to window 8 that said Patna,
and the clerk said go to window 13.
M went to window 13 and the clerk said go to window 8.
M found a train station manager who at first just said
he could not leave his post to show M where to go.
However, finally the manager did show M which
window to go to for buying the ticket to Patna.

On the train ride to Patna
M was talking with one of the other passengers.
He was an engineer and he told M
that he had a friend who had a hotel in Patna
and that he would show M where the hotel is.
The man spoke with a tricycle rickshaw driver
about transportation to the hotel.
The man translated the conversation to M
and said the rickshaw driver was wondering
why the man would not allow him
to charge the foreigner the foreigner's price.
M's experience in India was that rickshaw drivers
and others will charge a foreigner
ten to twenty times the price
that locals pay for the same service.

While riding in the rickshaw
M noticed fires burning in the street
and asked the engineer why that was.
The man immediately opened a large umbrella.
Until M mentioned those fires
the engineer forgot that this was Holi.
The next day is when people start throwing
colored water on each other.
Everyone is fair game, even foreigners.
M was not familiar with Holi.
The engineer showed M his friend's hotel
and asked his friend not to charge M
the foreigners price.
The price for the Hotel room was very low.
Around $2 USA per night.
The next day everyone was throwing colored water
on M's body and clothes.
The engineer had forgotten to explain
the throwing colored water part of Holi.
M was wearing white cotton clothes.
You are probably thinking
that it was only a little colored water.
They were pouring a full liter of colored water
on M's body and clothes all at one time.
One person poured a whole liter on top of M's head.
Another person poured a whole liter on M's shirt.
By the end of the day M had maybe 5 liters
of colored water poured on his body and clothes.
There was not even one patch of white left
on those white cotton clothes.

The next day M went to Bod Gaya.
The Holi celebration was still in effect
and M's second pair of white cotton clothes
got some color that day.

The place where Buddha sat while he practiced and then achieved Nirvana is called the Bodhi Tree.
The temple complex surrounding the Bodhi Tree is a peaceful place.
M was fortunate because there were no other visitors to the Bodhi Tree while M was there.
There are almost one billion Buddhists in the world, therefore to be the only person visiting the Bodhi Tree was an unexpected treat.
M picked up a leaf from the Bodhi tree and put it in a book.

Later there was a man who guided M to various places around that temple complex.
The guide showed M the places where the Buddha underwent various experiences before the Buddha made the decision that he would sit under the Bodhi Tree and not get up again until he had attained the final Freedom.

The guide said M was lucky to have found that leaf from the Bodhi Tree on the ground because the temple priests usually keep the leaves swept.
They sell those leaves and also give them away as gifts.

One time M visited Sarnath.
Sarnath is the place where Buddha first taught after he reached Nirvana under the Bodhi Tree.
Sarnath is near Varanasi.
The ancient Buddhist literature mentions the Buddha teaching at the deer park.
They had a small deer park there in Sarnath.

Both the trip to Bod Gaya and the trip to Sarnath were meaningful.
It was nice to see the place
where Buddha's Nirvana occurred
at the Bodhi Tree in Bod Gaya.
It was also nice to see Sarnath,
the place where the Buddha
first turned the wheel of the Dharma.

When M was in Sarnath
he had hired a tricycle rickshaw driver.
M asked the rickshaw driver
if he would allow M to drive the tricycle rickshaw.
The driver agreed.
Therefore the driver got into the passenger seat
and M attempted to pedal and steer
the tricycle rickshaw.
It seemed to be going OK at first.
Then the wheel turned to the right
and M was not able to stop the tricycle rickshaw
from going into a ditch.
Both M and the driver were OK
and there was no damage to the rickshaw.
However, the driver was very adamant at that point
that he and not M would be driving the rickshaw
from then on.
M agreed that would indeed be best.

While M was in Patna a Tibetan man
stayed at the same hotel M was staying at.
M was talking to the man
and the man explained that he lived in Nepal.
He was there in India to find a doctor for his brother
who had broken his shoulder.
M told the man I am going to Nepal.

The Tibetan man gave M his home address
which was in a Tibetan Refugee community
near Pokhara.
Because M was headed to Nepal next,
M thought he would be arriving
before the man got back to his home
and M told the man if you write a letter to your wife
to let her know you are OK
I will give the letter to your wife.
The Tibetan man wrote a letter to his wife in Tibetan.

As it turned out the Tibetan man
arrived back home before M arrived at his home.
The Tibetan man's wife spoke very good English.
The wife offered M some tea.
The wife asked M would Tibetan tea be OK?
M said yes.
However M was assuming Tibetan tea
would be like other tea.
It was not like other tea!
It was not what M would call tea!
Just imagine if you took a cup
and filled the cup one quarter full of butter,
and added one quarter cup of salt.
Then added hot water.
That was how this tea tasted!
M sort of pretended to be drinking the tea
because M did not want to offend his hosts.
The grandmother would come around
every five minutes to offer M more tea.
M said, no thank you
I still have more tea here in the cup.

There in Pokhara, Nepal
one time M was walking down a road headed downhill.
A European woman rode by on a bicycle.
As she rode by she said to M "NO BRAKES!"
She was going by M much too fast on that bicycle
downhill with no brakes for M to catch her.
However, catching her
would probably not have been a wise idea.
Let us suppose that somehow M could have
run after her bicycle fast enough to catch up to her,
and let us suppose that M grabbed unto
the back of her bicycle to slow her down to a stop.
That could have caused her to fall off the bike
and be either injured or even possibly cause death.
Therefore, the fact that M could not catch her
was probably a good thing.
Hopefully that woman found some way
to stop that bike without being injured.

M visited a place that had a lake
with a Buddhist temple on it in Pokhara.
M saw a group of Buddhist nuns visiting that place
while he was there.

In Nepal it is very common to see
Tibetan Buddhist Monks.
They are easily recognizable because
they are wearing maroon colored robes.

M had arrived in Pokhara on a bus.
There were a group of Americans traveling together
as part of a tour.
Maybe a group of students.
The leader of the group for some reason
spent some time talking to M.

When everyone got off the bus
there were a huge number of touts
from the various local hotels.
Seeing so many touts
trying to aggressively sell M something,
the leader of the group asked M
do you want to ride in the taxi we are taking
to our hotel?
M asked will you be staying in town or by the Lake.
The leader said we will be staying in town.
M told him thank you but I want to stay near the Lake.
It was nice of the leader of the tour to make the offer.

Katmandu Nepal has a very large population.
It also has a lot of westerners living there.
Nepal is an easier place to visit for a westerner
because they have so many westerners there,
they have the things a westerner would expect
for a comfortable place to live,
and the foods a westerner is used to eating,
and things that a westerner uses like toilet paper, etc.
Western style toilets are much more common in Nepal
than they are in India.

If you wonder
where did all the hippies from the 1960's go?
They went to Nepal.
Must be more than a thousand hippies living there.

There is a city not far from the Taj Mahal in India
called Fatehpur Sikri.
The tomb of the sufi Salim Chishti is there.
There was a picture of Pir Vilayat Inayat Khan there.
M recognized the picture because M had once
gone to a two week retreat with Pir Vilayat in the USA.
M felt a more powerful presence at the tomb
of Salim Chishti than he had ever felt any place else.

As far as a powerful *peaceful* presence goes the place
M felt that stronger than any place else was at Sringeri.
One of the four shankaracharyas is there.

FIRST TRIP TO SEE PAPAJI

The year might have been 1992.
M read a magazine article about a teacher who was
a disciple of Ramana Maharshi named Papaji.
(H.W.L. Poonja).
The magazine article was probably the article titled
Plunge Into Eternity in the September/October issue
of Yoga Journal by Catherine Ingram.
M decided to go to India as soon as possible
to see Papaji.
The fact that Papaji's guru was Ramana Maharshi
was part of the attraction for M.
To see a Self Realized Sage
whose guru was Ramana Maharshi
was a thrilling prospect for M.

Very early in December 1992
M was on his way to India to see Papaji.
M spent the night in Hong Kong.
On the television news M saw that
a mosque had been destroyed in Ayodyha, India.
That pins down the date because
that mosque was destroyed on December 6, 1992.
Therefore M probably arrived in India around
December 8 or 9 and M probably arrived in Lucknow,
the place where Papaji was,
around December 11 or 12, 1992.
M knew from the moment he saw on television
that Hindus had destroyed a mosque
that meant there was going to be trouble in India.
There was a curfew in Lucknow and also
M often saw trucks full of soldiers in Lucknow.

One year later the death toll from the violence
was more than 1000 people killed in India
due to the conflict
the destruction of the mosque in Ayodyha caused.

People had many experiences in front of Papaji.
It was decades later when M learned
that according to Papaji all those experiences were false
and that none of those people had attained Manonasa.
M was full of joy attending the satsang of Papaji.

Prior to January of 2004
M did not *know for sure* who *had* attained Manonasa
and who had *not* attained Manonasa.
M *thought* many teachers *had* attained Manonasa
who had *not* attained Manonasa.
One such teacher
who M *thought* had attained Manonasa
who in Reality had *not* attained Manonasa was:

RAJNEESH/OSHO

On a trip to India M spent 5 weeks in Poona
attending Talks given by Osho.
This was after Rajneesh had been to Rajneeshpuram
in the USA and he had changed his name to Osho.
If M had known about the crimes
that Ma Anand Sheela had been convicted of,
M would never have gone to Poona
to attend the Talks of Rajneesh/Osho.
However, M only learned about all of that later.
Rajneesh looked like a movie star
arriving in an expensive car and wearing sun glasses.
More than 5,000 people were attending the talks
of Rajneesh/Osho when M was there.

On one of M's trips to India he went to the place
where Nisargadatta Maharaj taught and lived.
Nisargadatta's body was no longer living,
however M was so impressed by the book I AM THAT
M wanted to see the place anyway.
The steps and stairs leading to the room
where Nisargadatta taught were very narrow.

One time in the USA
M and the ex girlfriend went to a state park.
Maybe it was around one hour driving time
from Santa Cruz, California.
M had brought a loaf of bread and some avocados
for the purpose of making avocado sandwiches.
M and the ex sat down at a park table.
Very far in the distance M saw a deer.
Maybe the deer was 500 or 700 feet away.
M took some bread and rolled it into a ball
and threw it in the deer's direction.
The bread probably only landed 50 or 100 feet towards
the deer which was still a long way from the deer.
The deer had seen M throw that bread.
The deer walked towards M and the ex girlfriend
and ignored the bread M had thrown.
The deer walked right up to M and M fed the deer.
After the deer had eaten half of the loaf of bread
the deer walked away.
By its actions the deer was communicating that
throwing bread on the ground is not the way to feed it.
The way is for the deer to walk right up to one
and one then feeds it by hand.
The deer was communicating that
it had no fear of humans.
The fact that the deer ate a half loaf of bread meant
the deer liked the bread, otherwise
the deer could have stopped at the first or second slice.

When the deer left it was communicating that
its belly was full and that half a loaf of bread is enough.
M loved the experience of feeding that deer.

One time in the USA
M saw some large bighorn sheep
by the side of the road.
M pulled over and fed the sheep some bread.
The sheep were very wild because
just the slightest movement of the knee
and they would back away.
M really enjoyed feeding those sheep.

For twenty years from body age 18 to body age 38
M operated the family business,
a small 26 room motel on the strip in Las Vegas.
Over that long period of time
usually M lived on the motel property
and there were three different places
M lived on that property at different times.

One of the places M lived was
a small studio apartment
that was next to the motel office.
One day M opened the door planning to go outside
and a black cat came inside the apartment.
M had never seen that black cat before.
The black cat looked around a little bit
and then went behind the sofa bed
into the small space between the sofa bed and the wall.
Later that same day the cat had kittens in that space.
Just imagine a cat you have never seen before
coming into your apartment, going behind the sofa
and a few hours later having kittens!

The motel next to the motel that M operated
was owned by a family from Taiwan.
They had a son
and the son's girlfriend bought him a dog.
The dog's name was Kiwi.
A strange name for an Australian Shepard.
The son's mother did not really like dogs
and was not pleased about that gift.

Kiwi stayed on an upstairs porch.
The porch had a gate.
A string was used between the two thin posts of the gate
to keep the gate closed.
Every day Kiwi would use her nose
to push up that string so that the gate was now open,
then Kiwi would climb down those stairs,
then Kiwi would come to the motel that M operated
and Kiwi would visit with M.
Kiwi probably sensed that the mother did not like dogs
and Kiwi probably loved being around M
because M loved Kiwi.
Animals are very aware and sensitive
to that sort of thing.
The mother noticed that Kiwi
had been escaping every day to visit M
so the mother asked M would you adopt Kiwi?
Therefore when Kiwi was around age 2 M adopted Kiwi.
Kiwi was a very kind, loving, gentle dog.

M already had a cat at the time of adopting Kiwi.
M had given the cat the name Pooky.
One of the employees of the motel that M operated
had found Pooky tied to a tree at a Hotel with no id tag.
The employee brought the cat back to the motel
and asked M would you adopt the cat?
M said yes.

When M brought Kiwi into the apartment
Pooky freaked out.
There was a cabinet around 10 feet high
and Pooky found a way to jump on top of that
and stayed there for a very long time.
It is amazing how a cat can show anger.
Pooky would look at M with such an angry face.
Not at Kiwi, at M!
Pooky knew who the traitor was
who had brought that dog into the apartment!
Eventually Pooky got over it
and got used to Kiwi living there.

One day a dog that M had never seen before
walked unto the motel property.
The dog was quivering with fear.
The dog put its head under M's arm.
The owner came soon and took the dog away.
M felt guilty for decades
for not having thought about a solution fast enough.
Later M realized he could have offered the dog owner
money for the dog and saved the dog from that owner
whose treatment of the dog was such
that the dog was quivering with fear
and looking for protection.

For most of those 20 years
M lived on the motel property in various locations.
However, from time to time he felt he needed a break
so that he did not live at the same location
where he worked.
He rented an apartment near the MGM Grand Hotel.
M opened his apartment door one day
not long after he had moved into that apartment
and a cat came in.
The cat had no collar and no id tag.
Later M gave that cat the name Prema.

Prema means love in Sanskrit.
Prema was a very affectionate cat
who loved to be petted.
Every day Prema would come into M's apartment
and visit M.
Prema did not sleep in the apartment.

One day when M returned to the apartment
from work, M noticed the window was broken.
A thief had broken in while M was at work.
M called the police.

Because of the break in
M decided to vacate the apartment
and move back to the motel.
When M carried the last package to his car for the move
from which he would never be returning
to the apartment,
Prema the cat jumped into the backseat of M's car.
This really surprised M
because M had never seen Prema in the parking lot.
The apartment was a second floor apartment
and M had only seen Prema come visit him
at his apartment.
Did Prema know that after loading the packages
M would never be returning?
If so, how could a cat know that?
Since Prema did not have a collar or a tag
M had a decision to make.
To take Prema with him
since he would never be returning
or to pick Prema up and set Prema outside the car.
M decided to take Prema with him back to the Motel.

After arriving at the Motel
as soon as M opened the car door Prema jumped out of the car and immediately spotted a pigeon on the bush planter and attacked the pigeon.
M grabbed the pigeon
and put the pigeon in his apartment.
The pigeon did not seem well enough to fly away.
So M had someone who worked at the motel
build an outdoor cage for the pigeon.
It took a few days for the pigeon to realize that
M was there to give it food and water and not to hurt it.
So one day after the pigeon had been in the cage
a few days M opened the door to the cage
and the pigeon flew unto M's shoulder.
That was the pigeon's way of saying
I know you are here to feed me, not to hurt me.

After around three months in the cage the pigeon seemed well enough to live on its own outside the cage.
M opened the door to the cage.
The pigeon was reluctant at first but eventually
the pigeon came out of the cage and flew away.
The pigeon was reluctant
because it had become accustomed to the cage as home after only three months.

With humans,
they are in the cage of the false self their entire lives.
It is almost impossible to convince humans
to come out of that cage and discover what Freedom is.

M'S LAST DAY AT THE MOTEL

The Motel was sold.
M immediately purchased a one way ticket to India
for the purpose of attending Papaji's satsang.

M's father had purchased that motel on the Strip
in Las Vegas and on July 7, 1967 M's family moved to
that motel when M's body was around 8 years old.
For 25 or 26 years out of the 30 year period
from July 7, 1967 to July 7, 1997
M had either worked or lived at that Motel.
A very strange coincidence is that
the last day M ever saw that motel was on July 7, 1997
exactly 30 years to the day
from when M's family had moved to that Motel.
It was nothing deliberate to make that exact coincidence
because the family had been trying to sell the motel
for four years before it finally sold.

On July 7, 1997 M carried the boxes to the car.
He was living in an apartment
attached to the motel office
and the route through the office
was easier than the side door
so M propped the motel office door open
and carried boxes from the apartment
to his car via the motel office.
While M was carrying one of those boxes
a pigeon flew into the motel office
and landed on the front desk counter.
The front desk counter is the place where customers
would go to rent a room, fill out a registration card etc.
The pigeon was not bothered by M walking past it
carrying the moving boxes.
In the last 30 years a pigeon had never before landed
on the motel front desk or flown into the motel office.

Therefore this pigeon landing there was very unusual.
M made a few more trips carrying boxes to the car
and when he was carrying the last box to the car
the pigeon flew outside of the office
and flew on the ground to be right next to M.
The pigeon wanted to be near M regardless
if M was carrying boxes through the office
or going to the car.

A question might arise was it the same pigeon
as M had the cage built for?
M had not seen the pigeon
that he had the cage built for in more than one year.
From the day M released that pigeon
M never saw that pigeon again.
Therefore, it would be just as miraculous
if it was the same pigeon or if it wasn't.
Did the pigeon know M was leaving the motel forever
that day and would never return?
If so, how could a pigeon know something like that?

All of the boxes were loaded into the car
and the pigeon was still there next to the car.
M finally convinced the pigeon to fly away.
Then M drove away from the Motel
headed for a mini storage unit
that he had previously rented.
M never saw the Motel again.
The Motel was later demolished by the new owner
who wanted the property for the land.

Later that same day, July 7, 1997
M boarded a flight to Los Angeles.
In Los Angeles he rented a motel room for a few days
for the purpose of resting before his flight to India.

The fact that M bought a one way ticket to India
for the purpose of attending Papaji's satsangs
and not a round trip ticket
is a great key to understanding M's motivations
and the way M centered his whole life
around Self Realization.
M intended to attend Papaji's satsangs
for as long as Papaji continued to have satsangs.
M thought that would be for many years.
That turned out not to be the case
because M arrived in Lucknow
around the 11th of July 1997
and had the privilege of attending Papaji's last satsangs.
Papaji's body passed away on September 6, 1997.

They brought Papaji's body into the Satsang Hall
(Satsang Bhavan).
M was one of the people who stayed there all night
until after the sun rose the next day.
M was crying on and off for around 12 hours.

M was planning to go to the cremation
of Papaji's body.
M talked with an autorickshaw driver.
People going to Papaji's cremation had left a temporary
shortage of rickshaws available
and this rickshaw was quoting M a price
that was around 40 times the normal price.
M decided he was not going to be taken advantage of
on this day, the day of Papaji's cremation.
Therefore M had decided to walk back
to the guest house where he was staying.
Within one minute of having
talked to that autorickshaw driver
and making the decision not to go to Papaji's cremation
a motorcycle drove by.

The driver of the motorcycle stopped
and asked M if he wanted to go to Papaji's cremation.
M said yes.
The motorcycle driver pointed to a white van
that was coming and said this was a relative of Papaji
and he can take you to the cremation.
The white van stopped and M was the only passenger.
The relative and M went to the cremation of Papaji.

There was something of interest
that M observed at the cremation of Papaji's body.
After two hours of fire, Papaji's body looked the same.
That was surprising because
there had been another cremation
of someone else that day
and M noticed that the entire cremation
from start to finish only took 2 hours.
Therefore, for Papaji's body to look the same
after two hours of fire was a surprise.
The fire for Papaji's body
lasted maybe around 4 or 5 hours.

David Godman was there at Satsang Bhavan
(the place where Papaji's satsangs occurred).
M had someone arrange for a meeting
with David Godman.
M met David Godman at the bookstore
there at Satsang Bhavan.
M asked David about Laksmana and Saradamma:
do they have a regularly scheduled satsang?
David said no they have never had that.
David said you can knock on their gate
and either they will let you in or they won't.
David said you can try writing to them,
however, that may or may not help
regarding them agreeing to meet you.

M asked David:
other than Laksmana and Saradamma
do you know of any other living teachers
who have realized the Self?
David said no, other than those two, no.

M decided to return to the USA
and go to Santa Cruz, California
to attend the Satsang of Nome and Russ.
M attended the satsang of Nome and Russ
for around three months.
M had volunteered to work in their bookstore
and M was working around 40 hours per week
in their bookstore as a volunteer.
This gave M some private meetings with Nome
from time to time to discuss the bookstore.

At one of the satsangs of Nome and Russ
M had an interesting experience.
M could feel a powerful laugh
that was arising from his belly.
M had never experienced anything like that before.
It was like a laugh
that actually had a huge force behind it.
M did not want to laugh there during satsang
because M did not think it would be appropriate
to burst out laughing while Russ was talking.
Therefore M had to use all his strength
to suppress that unusual laugh force that was arising.
Just then Russ said to the group assembled
this is not a Christian group
where you are not supposed to laugh
in the middle of the service.
That was quite amazing.
How did Russ know what was happening to M?

One time Nome was talking about
Adi Sankara's six aids to Self Realization.
I don't remember which aid he was talking about
but it probably was the subject of self control.
Nome used an example:
suppose you have a craving for ice cream.
All of the stores in Santa Cruz are closed.
Therefore, you drive all the way down to Monterey
to buy some ice cream.
That would be an example of lack of self control.
M made a joke and said "no need to get personal."

During that time
M had what he called Super Satsang Sundays.
M would attend Nome and Russ's satsang
in the morning.
Then M would drive two and a half hours to Marin.
Then M would attend Gangaji's satsang at 4:00 PM.
Thus the name Super Satsang Sundays.

On one of those Sundays
M began to experience unbroken continuous bliss
during Russ and Nome's satsang.
The bliss continued to intensify
on the drive from Santa Cruz to Marin.
M stopped in San Francisco to pick up the ex girlfriend
and take her to Gangaji's satsang.
The unbroken continuous bliss
continued to intensify during Gangaji's satsang.
After Gangaji's satsang
the ex girlfriend and M went to a pizza shop.
They had a salad bar
and therefore M chose the salad bar.
While eating some fresh spinach
M was telling the ex girlfriend
that the unbroken bliss that started in the morning
has been continuous and that even now it is continuing.

After three months
of attending the Satsang of Russ and Nome
M decided he wanted to stop seeing teachers
and just focus on turning within to the inner teacher.
M moved to Nevada and around six months later
in the summer of 1998
M bought a ten acre parcel of land that is very secluded
and that had a mobile home on it.
M got a bargain price.
He only paid $35,000 for that.
However, a few years later
he did have to purchase another used mobile home
because the one on the property had fallen apart.

At some point in time
someone who had spent more than 10 years
attending Nome and Russ's satsang sent M an email
that had a very large list of very terrible things
Nome and Russ had allegedly done over the years.
M knew how often rumors that are not true
get started about Sages, especially by ex students.
Therefore M decided to verify the accusations.
M knew another person who also had attended
Nome and Russ's satsang for over ten years.
M sent an email to that person
with the list of accusations about many things
Nome and Russ had done over the years.
The second person,
whom M had known for a very long time,
whom M knew could be relied upon to be truthful,
verified that the entire list of accusations about what
Nome and Russ had done over the years was true.
I will not give any details of what was on that very large
list of things Nome and Russ had done over the years.
I will just describe what categories those actions
by Russ and Nome over the years fall under:
1. Evil. 2. Vicious.

If M had known about those behaviors before,
M would never have attended
the satsang of Nome and Russ.

Because M had not yet attained Manonasa
he had no way to be certain of who had attained
Manonasa and who had not attained Manonasa.
M had believed many people had attained Manonasa
who had not attained Manonasa.
Gangaji is a good example of this.

M had not read or heard anything
that Papaji had said about his "ambassadors."
If M had heard or read what Papaji said
about his ambassadors,
including what Papaji said specifically about Gangaji,
M would never have attended the Satsang of Gangaji.

If you would like to know what Papaji had to say
about those he sent to teach
and also about those experiences
that so many people had
when attending Papaji's satsangs,
the book *Nothing Ever Happened*
(a three volume set) is a good place to start.

When asked about those he sent to teach,
Papaji said the purpose was
to have them point the way to Lucknow,
not to pose as awakened teachers.

Papaji said that many can fool others into
thinking they are liberated but they are the false coin.

When asked about the experiences
that so many people had in Lucknow,
Papaji said they were false experiences.

When asked
Why did you give them false experiences?
Papaji said to get the leeches off my back.

There is a short youtube video
titled Papaji Satsang: The fake messengers
where you can hear what Papaji said
on the subject of those teaching in his name.
The questioner asked about Issac, Andrew Cohen
and Gangaji.

WHAT CAUSED THE DESIRE FOR MANONASA TO BECOME TEN MILLION TIMES MORE INTENSE THEN LATER TO BECOME TRILLIONS OF TIMES MORE INTENSE

One of my students recently asked:
You mention how M the seeker's desire for Liberation
became 10 million times stronger
and eventually trillions of times stronger.
I am curious what insights, actions, life events etc...
led to this increase in M's desire.

To answer this question in detail
is going to take many pages.
It is worthwhile including the following very detailed
answer to that question in this autobiography.
The awakening of
the extremely intense desire for Manonasa
can also be called the extremely intense desire
to bring the ego and all suffering and sorrow to an end
and to remain eternally as the true Self
in perfect Awareness Love Bliss,
or it can be called awakening the
extremely intense desire for Freedom or Liberation.

The awakening of
the extremely intense desire for Manonasa
is the most important key
to attaining Manonasa.
The awakening of the
extremely intense desire for Manonasa
is like the light of the Sun
and all other keys to Manonasa
are only like the light of a light bulb compared to it.
The awakening of the
Extremely Intense Desire for Manonasa is everything,
it is the totality.
The extremely intense desire for Manonasa
will bring everything else that is needed.
The extremely intense desire for Manonasa
will bring extremely intense self honesty.
The extremely intense desire for Manonasa
will make you drop all of your unnecessary activities
and it will make you devote
all of the free time thus created to practicing
the most rapid and direct means to Manonasa.

What made that
Extremely Intense Desire for Manonasa
become ten million times more intense
and then trillions of times more intense is:

1. The extent to which the ego allowed M to see
each of the items on the list on pages 130 – 134.
The ego had allowed M to begin to see some of
the items on the list from body age 7 onward
to a greater extent than
the vast majority of humans ever see those listed items.
However,
the ego-mind was not allowing M to see
the full extent of the items on that list.

2. Seeing the items on that list first individually
helped greatly.
Then since all the items on that list
were pointing to the same truths,
seeing them as one collectively also helped.
However, seeing them individually
is what is most important
because “seeing them collectively”
is usually an ego preservation strategy
aimed at never really seeing them at all.
Instead of the expression “seeing them collectively”
it would be more accurate to say that
seeing them more clearly individually,
and seeing the extent of each item individually
was the main factor that led to the Desire for Liberation
becoming ten million times more intense
and then Trillions of times greater.
Seeing that all the items were pointing to the same
Truths is what is meant by seeing them collectively.

The list that follows
are some of the items the seeing of which,
and the extent to which the ego allowed M to see them,
was the cause for the
Awakening of the Extremely Intense desire for Freedom.
When that desire for Freedom became
trillions of times stronger
it was because of the extent to which
the ego allowed M to see all of those items.
The ego finally allowed M to see all of those items fully.

All of those items were pointing to the same truths:
The ego mind saw the need for
the ego mind to come to a final end
as soon as possible.
Ending the ego mind
was the only worthwhile action in life.

The following Truths are what the ego-mind
usually never allows a human to see
or if it does allow a human to see it,
it only allows a human to see
a tiny part of the extent of it
and not the full extent of it.
Seeing all of these Truths and the full extent
of each one of these Truths
was one of the primary factors that led to
the extremely intense desire for freedom to arise in M
and then to become trillions of times stronger.
Another factor was seeing that there is a solution
that will put an end to all this
and allow one to live eternally in bliss.
The solution is Manonasa
and the practice that leads to Manonasa.

HERE IS THE LIST OF 18 TRUTHS:

1. All ego's are evil.
That was the key difference.
As long as M thought that some ego's are not evil
that left the ego-mind enough hope
to not see the absolute need and urgency
of ending the ego-mind.
Until the ego-mind saw that 100% of ego-minds are evil,
Manonasa was impossible
and going to the ten million
and then trillions of times greater level
of the Desire For Freedom was also not possible.

2. All of human life
both that of spiritual seekers
and that of people
not interested in religion and spirituality
is a lie.

3. The only way that all sorrow and suffering can end
eternally is Manonasa.

4. The only way to remain as the True Self whose nature
is Absolutely Perfect Infinite Awareness Love Bliss
is through Manonasa.

5. Every moment of unnecessary activity in life
that could have been used towards practicing
the most rapid and direct means to Manonasa
is preventing Manonasa.

6. Achieving Manonasa requires a 100% commitment
that one's actions prove.

7. Attaining Manonasa
has nothing to do with Grace, Luck, Destiny, Fate,
some divine entities help, etc.
100% of the cause for attaining Manonasa
is your actions, your choices,
and what you do or don't do
including the actions you need to take to awaken the
Extremely Intense Desire for Freedom.
After Awakening
the extremely intense desire for Freedom,
the actions that the desire produces
such as dropping all of your unnecessary activities
and using all of the free time thus created
to read a small number of carefully selected
direct path books
and to practice the most rapid and direct method
for attaining Manonasa
are the causes for attaining Manonasa.
Also the intense level of self honesty
that the extremely intense desire for liberation brings
is a cause for Manonasa.
Self honesty begins
by actually catching your ego lying to you.
Catch your ego trying to lead you away from
this New Unique Direct Path to Manonasa.
An entire book of quotes by the Seven Sages titled
The Importance of Practice & Effort
was devoted to letting you know
it is your actions that are the cause of Manonasa
and that it is not grace, fate, destiny
or some divine deities help.

8. There have been more than 15,000 wars
in the last five thousand years.
Think of what each one of those hundreds of millions of
individual humans went through.
Think of how the billions of family members felt
knowing what happened to those millions of humans.
The deaths, the wounds, etc.
Humans are insincere
when they claim they want all this to end
because the only way for this to end
is by attaining Manonasa
and humans do not dedicate their lives
to attaining Manonasa.
When various solutions to a problem
have never succeeded in all of human history
the fact that humans do not try a truly new solution
demonstrates how
those thousands of layers of self-deception
actually love human problems including war.
This is part of the thousands of layers of self-deception
that the ego-mind almost never allows humans to see.
That is why after thousands of years of human history
the wars are continuing and will continue.

9. There is even more human violence
that does not occur in a war.
Homicides, and also physical violence
that does not end in death.
On whatever day you are reading this
more than a billion humans
will perform an act of violence
on more than a billion other humans.
Humans are insincere when they say
they want all this to end
because the only way this can end is Manonasa
and humans do not dedicate their lives
to attaining Manonasa.

10.. Billions of humans will perform an act
of verbal cruelty on other humans today,
the day you are reading this.
Humans are insincere when they say
they would like all this to end
because the only way for this to end
is Manonasa and humans do not
dedicate their lives to attaining Manonasa.

11. All humans lie to themselves every day.
Humans are insincere when they say
they want this to end
because the only way this can end
is by attaining Manonasa
and humans do not dedicate their lives
to attaining Manonasa.

12. Both what humans usually call evil
and what humans call good are evil.
See how the so called good supports the ego illusion.
See the ego motives in the so called good.
Only attaining Manonasa will end evil.

13. All of the spiritual and religious teachings
of the past are for the purpose of
preserving the ego-illusion.
The ego-illusion is the cause of all suffering, sorrow,
and evil.
Therefore, all of the spiritual and religious teachings
of the past are evil and are hurting humans.

14. When the ego-mind allows one to see the Truth
of even a small portion of this list of 18 Truths,
the doorway to Truth has opened a little.
When the ego-mind allows one to see the Truth of all of
these 18 Truths the doorway to Truth is wide open.

15. Since all of the perceived is temporary
it can never have any real meaning.
The only possible meaning in life
is to dedicate one's entire life to Manonasa.
When Manonasa occurs,
all suffering and all sorrow come to a final end
and what remains is the True Self which is
Infinite Eternal Awareness-Love-Bliss.

16. The ego-mind is thinking, thoughts, beliefs
and concepts
that are interested in preserving themselves.
They are not interested in the welfare of their host.
They are a parasite that is not concerned with
what harm they do to the awareness
that they have invaded.
They control the humans
and will not allow most humans
to see the truths on this list.

17. The language you think in
came from the outside,
that is why you had to learn it.
Something that came from the outside
now pretends to be your self and now controls you.
Thought is a kind of parasite
that is interested in its own welfare,
not your welfare.
The only solution to this is
to dedicate every second of your life
to attaining Manonasa.

18. Reading descriptions of
the nature of the True Self,
i.e. Infinite Eternal Awareness-Love-Bliss etc.
also helped M to awaken
The Extremely Intense Desire for Freedom.

Those 18 truths can be seen by anyone
in whom the desire for Truth and Freedom
is greater than the desire to continue the ego-mind.
The 18 items on the list are observations about humans
that can lead anyone to awaken
the extremely intense desire for liberation
if the ego will allow them to see those 18 truths.

The above list of 18 items are the primary factors
that led M to awaken
the extremely intense desire for Manonasa.
What follows are some of M's experiences in life
that also contributed to the awakening of
The Extremely Intense Desire for Manonasa:

M's experiences with so many other children
being cruel to M when M's body was a child also helped
to lead to The Extremely Intense Desire for Freedom.

M's experiences with
the total complete insincerity, and meanness of humans
during the 20 years he operated the motel in Las Vegas
also helped to increase M's desire for Manonasa.

When M spent time with spiritual seekers
in various groups in various locations,
usually those spiritual seekers were nice to M.
However, M could see that
all of those spiritual seekers in those various groups
were trying to preserve the ego-mind
and not really trying to bring it to an end.
M could see that even behind kindness
the ego's evil was still there.
That also helped increase M's desire for Manonasa.

M belonged to three online groups
that discussed spiritual subjects.
Each of those online groups
had more than 1000 members.
Two of the online groups had as their focus
the teachings of M's favorite Sage.
The other had a particular type of teaching
that has hundreds of different teachers as their focus.
The most evil M has ever read
were in those three spiritual groups.
All three of those groups
were pretending to be interested in spiritual teachings
that are for the purpose of
bringing the ego illusion to its final end.
**Almost every word posted in those groups
was for the purpose of
preserving the ego illusion**.

M had thought that it is understandable
that the people who stayed in the Las Vegas motel
were dedicated to the ego-mind,
and seeing the behavior of most of humanity
it is easy to see most of humanity
is dedicated to the ego-mind, however,
M thought that in at least some spiritual groups,
both those he visited in person
and also those online
there would be many people
who are not devoted to preserving the ego-mind.
It was a surprise for M to see that even in the spiritual
groups focused on the teachings of Direct Path Sages,
the real purpose of those groups
was to help each other preserve the ego-mind.

When Manonasa occurs, nothing human remains.
What remains after Manonasa occurs is not human.

The ego-mind will not allow most humans to see the truth of even one of the 18 items on the list.
Almost all humans who read the list of truths
are going to see the list of truths as a list of untruths.
Therefore you may be wondering
how is it possible to see these truths?
This is how you can see the 18 Truths:

1. Awaken the Extremely Intense Desire for Manonasa.

2. Be aware of your ego lying to itself.

3. Be aware of how your ego directs your thoughts, feelings and desires for the purpose of preserving its imaginary self.

4. See how your ego makes you spend time in unnecessary activities that will never lead to Manonasa.

5. If you can see the truth of even **one** of the 18 items that you did not see before,
you have cracked the door of truth open a little.
Once you see the truth of one item
you did not see before it is much easier to see the truth of the other items because you have created an opening.

Let us suppose that there is a spiritual teaching from the past or a spiritual group
that you thought was leading to Truth
and one day you see that teaching or group
is not leading to truth,
then you can begin to suspect
all of the spiritual teachings of the past.
Then you can ask what other items on the list
of 18 Truths might it be possible to see
even though you did not see them before?

I have joked with the student
who asked the question by telling him
that my detailed answer to his question
(the list of 18 items)
is going to double the number of negative reviews
this book receives.

I knew already
even while writing this autobiography
that this book was going to receive
a lot of negative reviews because of the ego-reaction.
However, the 18 item list which is the answer to
the student's question about what led the desire for
liberation to become trillions of times more intense
will probably double the number of negative reviews.
The human ego-mind is like a predictable machine,
if you push certain buttons
you are going to have certain reactions.

I decided that in writing this autobiography
I would not modify anything
in order to produce less of an ego-reaction in people.
Because:

1. Those one in a million spiritual seekers
who really do want to attain Manonasa
and are not lying to themselves
about wanting to attain Manonasa
deserve a book that tells the Truths
that almost no human is willing to see.
They deserve a communication
that has not been altered or modified
because of the ego-reaction it will cause.

2. Since most of the negative reviews
of the Eternal Bliss book,
under its many different titles and editions
had at least one item
that the person imagined was in the book
that was not in the book
and they criticized the book
based on what they had imagined,
people can be critical of an anti ego teaching
regardless if it is modified
to produce less of an ego reaction or not
by imagining things in the book
that are not in the book.
Some of the negative reviews were 100% imagination.

In this book the sentences and paragraphs
that are going to cause the most negative ego-reaction
and therefore negative reviews are obvious.
There are hundreds of such sentences
and in fact the entire book from beginning to end
is likely to produce such a negative ego-reaction
and negative reviews.

It would have been very easy
to just leave out or modify everything
that is going to cause the most negative ego reactions.
However, that would not have been fair
to that one in a million sincere spiritual seeker
who this book is being written for.

Fortunately, I learned from the experience
of all those different editions of the Eternal Bliss book
that even with many negative reviews,
there are still many people who see the value
and are not fooled by other people's ego reactions.

I never imagined when I created the Eternal Bliss Group that more than two thousand people would want to receive the quotes I send them. I thought the ego-reaction would prevent almost all people from wanting that. I thought that maybe one or two hundred people would become members of the Eternal Bliss Group. More than 2000 members was really a surprise.

There is a hidden rule. The rule is hidden in those thousands of layers of human self deception. The hidden rule is that all of the spiritual teachings that claim their aim is to bring the ego-illusion to an end are not for the purpose of bringing the ego-illusion to an end. The eternal bliss book and the book you are now reading breaks that rule, and those hidden layers of self deception are not going to like that rule having been broken.

There were many other life events and factors that led M to finally attain Manonasa. This entire autobiography from beginning to end describes that.

CHAPTER FIVE

WHEN THE BODY WAS IN ITS FORTY'S

In 2001 M made another trip to India.
M had a private meeting with A.R. Natarajan
in Bangalore.
Natarajan had published more Ramana Maharshi books
than anyone else with the exception of
Sri Ramanasramam.

A. R. Natarajan asked M:
"Is your father interested in
the Teachings of Ramana Maharshi?"

M said to Natarajan:
"The father of this body loves me.
Therefore he has always allowed me to read to him.
I have read the Teachings of Ramana Maharshi
to the father of this body many times.
I do not think that the father of this body
is interested in the Teachings of Ramana Maharshi
because every time I have read
the teachings of Ramana Maharshi
to the father of this body
in less than five minutes
the father of this body has been sound asleep."
Then M imitated the puffed cheeks
of the father's breathing while snoring.
Natarajan got a good laugh out of that.
M wanted to go to Sringeri next.
M asked Natarajan if Natarajan could find a taxi driver
to take him from Bangalore to Sringeri.
Natarajan made those arrangements.

Adi Sankaracharya established
four spiritual school locations in various parts of India.
Sringeri is one of those.
Adi Shankaracharya selected the Sringeri site
as the place to stay and teach his disciples,
because when he was walking by the Tunga river,
he saw a cobra with a raised hood
providing shelter from the hot sun
to a frog about to spawn.
Impressed with the place where natural enemies
had gone beyond their instincts,
he stayed there for twelve years.

Sringeri had the most peaceful presence
of any place M had ever been anywhere in the world.
M could feel that powerful peaceful presence
even before getting out of the taxi.
M was not sensitive to sensing presences
and therefore usually M never sensed anything.
M got some bags of puffed rice to feed the fish
there at Sringeri.
There was a family with a child there.
M gave one of the bags of puffed rice to the child
so that he could feed the fishes.
The family spoke to the child
in whatever their native language was
and probably told the child to take the bag
and to feed the puffed rice to the fish
because that is what the child did.
M never went across the bridge
to meet the living Shankaracharya.

After Sringeri M went to Tiruvannamalai
for the purpose of attending V. Ganesan's Talks
at his home called Ananda Ramana.
V. Ganesan is the grand nephew of Ramana Maharshi.

V. Ganesan was the editor of
Sri Ramanasramam's magazine (The Mountain Path)
for decades.
V. Ganesan interviewed
more than 400 devotees of Ramana Maharshi.

When M arrived there at Ananda Ramana
there was no Talk going on that day.
However Ganesan was there
and a man was there who is the editor of a magazine.
Maybe the magazine is called Tattvaloka.
The man is from Madras.
The magazine is for the purpose of publishing
the teachings of the Shankaracharya of Sringeri.
M had just come from Sringeri
and that was the only trip to Sringeri
that M had ever made.
The man from Madras
only rarely made visits to Ananda Ramana.
Spiritual life is full of amazing coincidences like that.
Those of you who are reading this book
have probably noticed
that when you are focused on the spiritual life
the number of unlikely coincidences that happen
is greatly increased.
Ganesan was wondering
how M became interested in Ramana Maharshi.
M explained the unlikely way
that M had found that Ramana Maharshi book at age 15.
The man from Madras said that M
had probably had some past life connection
to Ramana Maharshi.
Ganesan wanted to know what M's name is.
M said Mike.
Ganesan said "Michael."

M attended Ganesan's Talks every day.
Ganesan had a habit of always speaking to one person,
even though there may be 20 people there.
Every day Ganesan would look at the same person
and say their name over and over in the Talk,
as though he was only speaking to that one person.

When M started attending Ganesan's Talks,
every day Ganesan would look at M and say "Michael"
repeatedly.
That combined with the fact that
Ganesan had said Michael when M said Mike
led M to make the decision from that point forward
to always go by the name Michael instead of Mike.

Ganesan could read every sentence
in M's Mind.
Ganesan was the only person M ever met
who could read every sentence in M's mind
with perfect 100% detailed accuracy.
The same perfect accuracy
that one has when reading a book.
Only M and Ganesan knew what was happening because
only M and Ganesan knew what M's thoughts were.
On average four times during the Talk
Ganesan would say an exact thought that M had.
Sometimes it was a thought that M had during the Talk
and sometimes it was a thought M had the previous
evening or in the morning before the Talk.
When Ganesan would mention a thought that M had
the previous evening or in the morning before the Talk
**it was always at the first opportunity
for Ganesan to have spoken to M.**
In other words Ganesan never read a thought
that was two days old or three days old.
It was **always** the **first** time M was seeing Ganesan
after having had the thought.

Often these thoughts that M had that Ganesan read
had nothing to do with any spiritual Talk.
Sometimes they were very detailed thoughts.

Here is an example,
On a morning when M would be going
to one of Ganesan's Talks
while M was still in his guest house room
M had many thoughts about the conditions in India:
Garbage thrown everywhere
so that one was always walking past garbage,
and open sewers.
Omnipresent bribery,
Medical Doctors who paid a bribe
to get their medical degree.
People pretending be medical doctors
and practicing medicine
who did not actually have a medical degree.
Doctors pretending to be trained in a medical specialty
who were not trained in that specialty.
M was not happy about all the people
who had tried to cheat him while in India.
Any lie to make a sale would do.
Also M was thinking:
"How do these people think that these simple lies
are going to fool me?
I am from a country that put men on the moon, etc."

Then M went to Ganesan's Talk.
Ganesan said while looking into M's eyes:
Putting men on the moon is evolution.
What really matters is involution.
You can gloat over the fact that material conditions
are better in your country.
That is evolution.
What really matters is involution.

M's thoughts that morning had not even been on a spiritual topic.
Ganesan never spoke about
putting men on the moon before.
The **same morning** when M had those thoughts,
the exact same precise thoughts,
not just the men on the moon part of the thought,
the whole, entire complete thought
Ganesan read perfectly.

Ganesan read M's thoughts, exactly, precisely
no matter how obscure the thought was,
even when the thought had nothing to do with
anything Ganesan had said during his Talks.
Ganesan read M's mind around 4 times per day,
every day.
More than 50 times Ganesan had read
the exact, precise thoughts M had.

M was in his room
at the Sesha Bhavan guest house.
In the evening M had a rock from Arunachala
and held it in his hand.
With the rock in his closed hand
M waved the rock around.
M had never done that before.
The next morning Ganesan said to M
while looking into M's eyes:
You can take a rock from Arunachala
and hold it in your hand.
Then Ganesan demonstrated waving the hand around.
The Sesha Bhavan guest house
is near Sri Ramanasramam.
It is not anywhere near where Ganesan lives.
Ganesan had no way of knowing that the night before
M held that Arunachala rock in his hand
and waved it around.

Just imagine what it was like
to have that sort of precision in mind reading
done more than 50 times!
This was nothing like what the so called psychics do.
Those so called psychics have hits and misses
and more often than not they are talking in generalities.
With Ganesan it was absolute precision,
just like someone who can read a complex sentence
from a book word for word with 100% accuracy.

The owner of the Sesha Bhavan guest house
was also the owner of the Vallalar temple
on the circle route around Arunachala.
The owner of the temple wanted to put one large and
nine smaller Shiva lingams in a new room at the temple.
Nine different people each donated money
to pay for each of the nine lingams.
M was one of those people.
I do not know which of those nine lingams
was the one M sponsored.
Maybe the one with a smile.

At the Sesha Bhavan guest house
there was an upstairs area
that the owner of the guest house
would allow various western satsang gurus to use.
M happened to be there in that area all alone
when the area was not in use when the owner arrived
with one of the western satsang gurus
in order to show him the meeting area.
The owner of the guest house introduced the man
by saying this is a satsang guru.
Both the western satsang guru and M laughed
at that introduction.
M did not attend the satsang guru's satsang.

M had had enough of the new satsang gurus,
none of which have attained Manonasa,
to last a lifetime.
After attending the satsang of Gangaji, Nome and Russ
in 1997, M never attended the Satsang
of any of the new breed of Satsang gurus again.

One day M went upstairs to go to that
meeting area and a large group of monkeys was there.
Maybe 20 monkeys.

THE DISCOVERY OF THE AWARENESS WATCHING AWARENESS METHOD

By the year 2001 M had been studying
the teachings of almost all of the various religious
and spiritual paths for 27 years.
M had read more than two thousand spiritual books.
M had received instruction from many spiritual teachers
in America and India.
Far more spiritual teachers
than have been mentioned in this autobiography.

It was clear that
the essence of most spiritual teachings
was focusing the attention on the "I AM."
The place where "Hinduism," Buddhism, Judaism,
Christian Mysticism and Sufism meet is
turning inward and focusing the attention on "I AM."
The most direct and rapid means to eternal bliss,
finding the kingdom within, "Self-realization," Nirvana,
etc., is turning the attention within to focus on "I AM."

One modern example of this in "Hinduism"
is Nisargadatta Maharaj.
Nisargadatta's teacher (guru) told him
to pay attention to the "I AM" to the exclusion of all else.
Nisargadatta practiced
focusing his attention on the "I AM" for three years.
After three years of practicing in his spare time,
Nisargadatta realized his true Self.
Nisargadatta had to work to support his family;
therefore, he could only practice in his spare time.
Nisargadatta spent hours each day
looking at the true Self.

Focusing the attention on "I AM,"
is an ancient "Hindu" practice.

In Zen Buddhism
focusing the attention on "who is looking"
is found in the teachings of Master Bassui.

In Tibetan Buddhism
focusing attention on awareness is found
in some of the Dzogchen practice instructions.

The importance of looking inward
and knowing the "I AM"
is also found in the Judeo-Christian teachings:
"And God said to Moses, I AM THAT I AM.
And He said Thus you shall say to the children of Israel,
I AM has sent me to you" (Exodus 3:14).
"Be still and know I AM God" (Psalm 46:10).
"Jesus said, Before Abraham was, I AM" (John 8:58).
"Jesus said, The Kingdom of God is within you"
(Luke 17:21).
Jesus did **not** say,
Will be within you after your body dies.
Jesus said **is**. "Is" is present tense. "Is" is now.

The Prophet Mohammad said,
"He who knows his Self knows his Lord."
Self-cognition is a Sufi practice.

There are many other spiritual traditions
and teachings that have pointed out that
focusing the attention on the "I AM"
is the most direct and rapid means to Freedom
(i.e. Know thyself).

Another modern example from "Hinduism"
is Ramana Maharshi.
Ramana Maharshi taught for more than 50 years
that the only effective means to end the ego
and suffering and to remain as eternal joy
is to focus on the Self, the I, the I AM.

By the year 2001, M had attempted to practice
the method of focusing the attention on the "I AM"
for 27 years.
M had made very little progress with that method
or any other method.

In December of 2001 M was in Tiruvannamalai.
M was alone in his room
at the Sesha Bhavan guesthouse.
M was thinking about all the possible meanings of "I"
and "I AM" and all the possible approaches to
"I" and "I AM" that he had read about over the years:
The "I thought," the thought I AM.
The "I feeling," the feeling I AM.
The "I" consciousness," the "I AM" consciousness.
To think I or I AM.
To feel I or I AM.
To focus the attention on I or I AM.
Many different combinations of approaches
and the different views of what "I" or "I AM" means.

After 27 years, M was still not sure
what "I AM" means in direct experience.
M was wondering if there was some way
to solve these questions and to have clarity
both in the meaning of I or I AM
and in how to approach it;
whether to focus the attention on I AM,
or feel I AM, or think I AM, or...?

M wanted an understanding that was so clear,
there would be nothing vague remaining,
no more choices remaining.
M really wanted to know the answer.
M was not going to confine the answer
to any previous understanding.
M was willing to have his previous understanding
shattered, if necessary.
There was a willingness to consider the possibility
that for the last two and a half decades,
M had not understood at all what the "I AM" is
or how to focus on it.
It was a willingness to allow all the old views
and assumptions to be swept away, if necessary.

Ramana Maharshi had said Self-inquiry
is more like **feeling** than like thought.
Asking "Who am I?"
or asking "To whom do these thoughts arise?"
are easy instructions to follow
as long as one stays in the realm of thought.
However, when it comes to **feeling** "Who am I?"
or **feeling** "I AM",
the instructions had always been vague.
What exactly is the feeling "I AM?"
Of course a spiritual seeker can **imagine** that a
particular feeling is the same feeling as the Sages
are referring to when they say "I" or "I AM."

Of course a spiritual seeker can **believe**
that a particular feeling is the same feeling
that the Sages are referring to
when the Sages say "I" or "I AM"
however, it may be that **none** of the hundred different feelings that a hundred different spiritual seekers have
when they refer to the feeling "I" or "I AM"
are the same feeling that the Sages are referring to
when the Sages talk about the feeling of "I" or "I AM."

Nisargadatta Maharaj and many others had said the "I AM" is consciousness.
M wondered: "Is the 'I AM' the 'I *thought*'
or is the 'I AM' just my present *awareness*?"

M thought:

"If the 'I AM' is this present awareness,
the awareness that is now looking at this room,
then paying attention to the 'I AM' is just:

My present awareness
watching my present awareness.

This was a revelation!
Instead of having some vague practice
where one is told to pay attention to the "I AM"
without ever being sure exactly what the "I AM" is
and what it feels like,
here was an absolutely clear instruction:
My present awareness
watching my present awareness.

Not some unknown,
seemingly far away awareness
labeled the Infinite Self
or labeled God.

This awareness, my awareness,
here and now watching itself,
while ignoring thought, the body, the world, etc.

Immediately M tried this practice:
Turning the attention away from thought and towards awareness watching awareness.
M shut his eyes,
because the point was to ignore the world.
To turn the attention that normally goes out
into the world around 180 degrees and to look inward.
To turn the attention away from thoughts, feelings
and desires and towards awareness watching awareness.
If M noticed a thought, he ignored the thought
and brought the attention back to
awareness watching awareness.
Awareness paying attention to awareness
to the exclusion of all else.
Awareness paying attention only to itself.

The results were instant!
From the very first moment one tries this practice,
one is abiding as awareness!
There is no waiting!
It is easy.
This is not meant to imply
that from the beginning the ego ends.
It takes years of continuous practice
before the ego meets its final end.
However, from the moment one tries
this easy to understand practice,
one is being as awareness!

M practiced the
Awareness Watching Awareness Method for two years,
from December 2001 to January 2004.

There were more days with twelve hours of practice
than days with two hours of practice.
In January 2004 M's ego, sorrow and suffering
came to its **final end**,
and what remained is
Infinite-Eternal-Awareness-Love-Bliss.
In January of 2004 M attained Manonasa.
In some traditions Manonasa is called Nirvana,
Mukti, Moksha or Self Realization.
In January of 2004 the human dream
came to its **final end**
and the dream of a universe also came to its **final end**.

In January of 2004 the imaginary cycle
of births and deaths, also known as samsara,
came to its **final end**.
Thus the Awareness Watching Awareness Method once
again lived up to its reputation as being the most rapid
and direct means to Manonasa in this lifetime.

Ramana Maharshi and Nisargadatta Maharaj
had both specifically described the
Awareness Watching Awareness Method;
however M's ego did not allow him
to pay attention to those quotes.
The Awareness Watching Awareness Method
was like a buried treasure,
hidden among so many other quotes
on so many different subjects.
In the Step Seven quotes from the book
The Seven Steps to Awakening you can read the way
Nisargadatta Maharaj, Sadhu Om, Ramana Maharshi,
Sankara, Vasistha, Annamalai Swami and Muruganar
described the Awareness practice.

M was not the only one
who was ignoring those quotes.
In 2002 before M began posting on the internet
about the practice of awareness observing awareness,
M did an internet search using as many different ways
of describing the awareness observing awareness
practice as he could think of.
The search produced only three results.
Before M began posting at various online groups
the various ways the seven Sages had described
the practice of awareness observing awareness,
those quotes were almost never being posted.
People almost always preferred to post other quotes.
The ego-mind knows how to ignore the quotes
that are the greatest threat to it.
The ego-mind also knows how to pay attention
to the quotes that are the least threat to it.

Another reason that previously
M did not realize the true meaning of I AM
is that he had read that the "I AM," the true Self,
is infinite continuous awareness.
That made it seem like the "I AM"
must be something different from the awareness
that **appears** to wake up in the morning.
However, the habit of always looking outward
is what causes the awareness to **appear**
to wake up in the morning and to **seem** limited.
The awareness does not really wake up in the morning
and the awareness is not limited.
Waking up, going to sleep and limitation are illusions
created by the habit of always looking outward.
If one observes the awareness for many years,
eventually one discovers that
the awareness is continuous
and that it is not limited.

The significance of the
Awareness Watching Awareness discovery
is one of communication.
A human could be told to focus on the I AM
and even after one hundred million imaginary lifetimes,
still **not** know what the I AM is in practice,
while telling themselves and believing
that they do know in practice what the I AM is.
However, if told the I AM is the awareness
that **appears** to wake up in the morning,
the background of awareness
that is there during all the waking hours,
and given specific instructions
in how to turn the attention away from thought, etc.,
and towards awareness watching awareness,
one can permanently end the ego and suffering
in this lifetime and remain eternally in bliss.
The specific instructions are Chapter Seven
in the book *The Direct Means to Eternal Bliss.*
Chapter Seven is ten pages of very specific,
very detailed instructions.

2002 TRIP TO INDIA

In 2001 M asked Ganesan
if he would still be giving Talks at Ananda Ramana
next year when M would be returning to India.
Ganesan said yes.
However, that turned out not to be correct.
When M returned to India in 2002
Ganesan was not giving any talks at Ananda Ramana.

On this trip to India
the guest house that M was staying in
was probably called Arunachala guest house.
It is not far from Sri Ramanasramam.

One day at Arunachala guest house
M wanted to go downstairs
and a monkey was coming up the stairs.
Probably M should have just waited,
however M was filled with joy
and decided to go down the stairs
while the monkey was going up the stairs
which meant that M and the monkey
were going to be very close to each other
when they passed each other on the stairs.
M knew that many animals consider it a challenge
if you look them in the eyes, therefore,
M did not look the monkey in the eyes
while going down the stairs.
When M passed the monkey
the monkey snarled at M, however,
M just ignored the monkey
and continued down the stairs and it all turned out well.

M went to hear a talk by Lakshmana Swami.
It was a very small group
and M was sitting in the third row.
M was very close to Lakshmana Swami.
Lakshmana Swami spoke so softly
M could not hear even one word.
They had no chairs and therefore
the pain of sitting crossed legged was quite great.
One time M waited at Lakshmana Swami
and Saradamma's gate
just to get a glimpse of Lakshmana Swami
when he drove by.

One time M went to see Sadhu Om's Samadhi.
Another time M went to see
Annamalai Swami's Samadhi.

One time M climbed to the top of Arunachala.
At other times M meditated at various caves
on Arunachala.

One time M hired a man
who worked at Yogi Ramsuratkumar ashram
to help him with various things.
The man wanted M to meet the president of
Yogi Ramsuratkumar ashram
who was a retired supreme court justice.
M had a private meeting with the president.
The president told M
that he was not really a spiritually oriented person
and therefore he did not understand why
Yogi Ramsuratkumar chose him to run the ashram.
M said to the president that running an ashram
involves one in many worldly affairs.
It also poses many legal challenges.
Asking a retired supreme court judge to run the ashram
is a brilliant decision by Yogi Ramsuratkumar.

One time M did an
autorickshaw Giripradakshina of Arunachala.
To translate that into English for you:
Giripradakshina is usually done on foot.
It is going all the way around Arunachala mountain.
An autorickshaw is a three wheeled vehicle
with a motor.

THE PINK HOUSE

There was a new unoccupied pink house
around five minutes walking from Ganesan's home
Ananda Ramana.
M had thought that eventually someday V. Ganesan
will be talking again and M wanted to move to India
so that he could always attend all of Ganesan's talks.
So M decided to rent the pink house
and also to add many things to the pink house that
would be needed before moving into the pink house.

For example the pink house had no water.
There were a number of options for how to get water.
M preferred the option of digging a well.
Ananda Ramana had a well,
a house even closer to the pink house
and close to Ananda Ramana had a well.
On the other side of the pink house
there was a man who also had a well.
Therefore since there was water all around
it seemed a well could reach water at the pink house.

A man was called out to double check
to make sure that there was water
and where to dig for it before calling the well digger.
They called the man an engineer.
The so called engineer's method of determining
if there was water and where the water was,
was to walk around the property with a wrist watch
and shake that wrist watch many times.
To call a man who is using the method
of shaking a wrist watch
to discover the location of water an "engineer"
would be considered a joke in America.
The man said yes there is water
and gave the exact spot where the well should be dug.

Therefore the well drilling company was called.
They brought a truck out and plenty of pipe
in case the well would have to be very deep.
The owners of the pink house and M
stayed there all night long
watching the man drill the well.
After around 12 hours of drilling
the man said the well had been dug.

M was paying for all of the home improvements
including the well in exchange for credit on future rent.
The owners bought a pump for the well.
After installing the pump the well would only produce
one bucket of water in a 24 hour period.
The man who was working for M had told M that
the next morning after the well had been dug
someone had written something next to the well
to warn us that we had been cheated,
that there was no water.

Therefore M went to plan B.
Plan B was to dig a hole in the ground
and put in a tank to hold water.
Then a truck could deliver water to the house.
M also put a big water tank on the roof of the house.
It was a nice house.

M purchased two air conditioners
and a refrigerator in Tiruvannamalai.

M was going to make a trip to Pondicherry
for the purpose of purchasing a bed, a mattress,
a sofa and a metal cabinet.
The day before the trip M had laryngitis.

M had never believed in signs or omens,
therefore M did not realize that life was giving M
many signs or omens
that M should not make that trip to Pondicherry.
The laryngitis was one of those signs or omens.
M had never before had laryngitis in his life.

On the day of the trip
M was disappointed to see who the taxi driver was.
M had that same taxi driver previously
on a trip to Madras.
There in Madras that taxi driver kept parking
where he was not supposed to park.
One time that resulted in the police putting a lock on
the wheel of the taxi that required a fee to be removed.
Another time the taxi driver drove off
while a man was tapping on the taxi
trying to collect a small 5 rupee parking fee.
The taxi driver was not of good character.

M had also hired a truck for the trip
to Pondicherry so that the sofa, and bed, etc.
could be brought back to Tiruvannamalai.

In Pondicherry M was not able to find a bed
or a mattress that he wanted to purchase.
The only thing he found was the large metal cabinet.
A policeman detained the taxi driver in Pondicherry.
The policeman wanted 300 rupees
to release the taxi driver.
This was strictly a bribe because the policeman
was asking for this fee at night, under a tree,
and no paperwork was ever issued.
300 rupees was only around $6.00 US at that time,
so M paid the fee.

So the truck and the taxi began the drive
from Pondicherry back to Tiruvannamalai.
The taxi followed the truck.
It was at night.
M was in the taxi.
At some point in the journey
M was looking at the metal cabinet on the truck ahead
and M saw something very strange.
The wind was blowing the paper
that the metal cabinet was wrapped in
into shapes of a sinister looking character.
It was so detailed that it would have taken
a cartoon animator hours
to draw so many details of the character.
It was a very scary looking thing.
That was the only time in M's life
that M had ever seen anything like that.
M never had any visions in his life.

One of the people traveling in the taxi with M
saw what was happening on the truck and said:
"A ghost is dancing on the truck."
That means that he saw it too!
M had not thought of the word ghost
for that scary character
because M had never seen a ghost before.
That ghost was the third or forth omen or sign.
The first omen or sign was the laryngitis.
The second omen or sign
was seeing that same taxi driver
who had the bad character
show up for the drive to Pondicherry.
The third omen or sign
was the scary ghost dancing on the truck.

You could count the bribe having to be paid
to the policeman in Pondicherry as an omen
or sign also because if M had refused to pay the bribe
the taxi could not have left Pondicherry
and M would have been riding in the Truck
and the taxi would not have had the accident.

Maybe around 20 or 30 kilometers from
Tiruvannamalai the taxi driver was driving faster.
Maybe he wanted to get back home.
The taxi driver fell asleep
and drove into a concrete pillar.

In America M always wore a seat belt.
However the seat belt in this taxi was not working
therefore M was not wearing a seat belt.
There were no airbags in the taxi
because automobiles were not required to have airbags
in India.

M was sitting on the front seat.
Therefore M was only two feet from the driver.
M could not walk after the accident,
so M crawled on the ground.

Less than three hours after the accident
the taxi driver's body was dead.
M's face had hit the glass in the windshield,
therefore M had glass all over his face.
M had a pelvic bone fracture, a broken finger,
and broken ribs.

M was taken to a state hospital.
In India there is no cultural taboo against staring at
someone and therefore that often happens in India.
Many people in the hospital would stare at M
and still be staring at him 10 minutes later.

M's left leg had swollen
and they decided to make many incisions on the leg
to drain the fluid.
At the state hospital they had taped M's broken finger
the correct way.
M went two days without seeing a doctor again
or a specialist and therefore M decided
to check out of the state hospital.

M rented a room at a hotel.
However later that evening M's body began to stiffen
to the point where M could not walk.
Therefore M called the front desk
and had them send a doctor to the room.
The doctor told M you need to go to a medical clinic
and stay there until you heal up.
Therefore an ambulance was called
to transport M's body to the clinic in Pondicherry.

M was at that clinic for two weeks.
One day a nurse came into M's room
and said she was going to give M an injection.
M said to the nurse what is in the injection?
What is the purpose of the injection?
The nurse said she did not know.
M told the nurse he was not going to have an injection
until he had all of that information.
Later M saw the same nurse and reminded her that she
was going to get the information about the injection.
The nurse said the doctor said
the injection was supposed to be given to
another patient, not to you.

The brother of M's body knew a man in India
and asked that Man to go and visit M
in the clinic in Pondicherry.
That man told M that the person at the clinic
who is representing himself as an orthopedic doctor
has never been trained in that specialty.
The man told M that M should be transported to
a hospital in Madras to receive good medical care.

It is difficult to make good decisions
when one is laying in bed in a clinic unable to walk
with so very many injuries.
Therefore M decided to stay in the Pondicherry clinic.

The broken ring finger
was bent towards the pinky finger.
At the Pondicherry clinic they taped the ring finger
together with the pinky finger.
At the state hospital they had taped the ring finger
to the middle finger.
M told the doctor at the Pondicherry clinic
about the difference.
The doctor assured M that the way they were doing it
there at the Pondicherry clinic was the correct way.
In fact it was not the correct way.

After M had been in the Pondicherry clinic
for two weeks the brother of M's body flew from
America to India to help M get back to America.
The last time M was in India was in 2002.
After leaving that clinic in Pondicherry
M never went back to India.

On the flight to America the brother of M's body
told the flight attendant
that of the two brothers he was the more handsome.
This simply is not true! M's body was more handsome!

Back in America M checked into a hospital.
Three days and ten thousand dollars later
M checked out of the hospital.

The father of M's body had rented an apartment
for M in the same complex where the father lived
there in Las Vegas to provide a place for M to heal.
The place where M's home was
has so few people that there are almost no services.
Also M's home had steps which would have been
impossible in the condition of M's body.
Therefore the apartment was a much better place
for M to heal.

M was in a wheelchair
because the doctors did not want M to walk
until the pelvic fracture had healed.
They also told M to use a walker
if the wheel chair would not fit some place.
The walker had a special hand post on it
so that M's broken finger could remain motionless.
M was in that apartment for three months.
After three months everything in M's body had healed
except for the broken ribs.
The ribs took a little longer to heal.
Now M could walk without having to use a wheelchair
or a walker for the first time in three months.
The entire time M was there in that apartment healing
M continued to practice the
Awareness Watching Awareness Method.

M moved back home and continued to practice
the Awareness Watching Awareness Method.

CHAPTER SIX

MANONASA

In January of 2004 M attained Manonasa.
In this chapter a great amount of detail will be used
to convey to you what Manonasa is.
First what it is like just before Manonasa happens.
Then what Manonasa is.
Humans find it very difficult to understand
that the body and the world and universe disappear
at the moment of Manonasa
and never come back again in all of eternity.
One of the things that make that difficult
for the humans to understand
is because they see the body of a Sage
who has attained Manonasa functioning normally,
walking, talking, answering questions etc.
How can he talk if he has no perception of a body?
Therefore, many sources will be drawn upon
to explain Manonasa to you.
Quotes by the Seven Sages from the book
The Seven Steps to Awakening will be written here.
Stories from the book *The Direct Means to Eternal Bliss*
will be written here.
Ways that I have taught students
the meaning of Manonasa will be written here.

We will begin with looking at what happens
just prior to Manonasa.
There is a doorway to Manonasa.
It is not a physical doorway.
The word doorway is being used as a vehicle
to communicate something to you.
Not even one out of every ten million humans
reaches the doorway to Manonasa.

In other words even to reach the *doorway* to Manonasa
is extremely rare.

Of those humans
who do reach the doorway to Manonasa
almost none of them goes through that doorway.
That is why less than one out of every
five hundred million humans attains Manonasa.
All humans who reach the doorway to Manonasa
are afraid to go through that door.
Even those very few who do go through that door are
afraid before they go through the door to Manonasa.
The reason they are all afraid is
the ego-mind knows that if it goes through that door
it will come to its final end.
The only identity a human knows is that ego-mind.
The person may have read in books
you are not the ego-mind you are the True Self
hundreds of times.
However, that reading does not change the fact
that they are still identified with the ego-mind
and their experience is that the ego-mind is their self
even though it is not their real Self in reality.
The reality is not what a human is experiencing.
What a human is experiencing is the dream
and in that dream the only self they are experiencing
is the false self or ego-mind.
Thus it *appears* to the human
that if they go through that door they will cease to exist.
The Truth is if they go through that door
the ego-mind will cease to exist,
all suffering and sorrow will end forever,
the universe will disappear forever and never reappear,
the body will disappear and never reappear.
However, they will still exist as the True Infinite Self.

However, it does not seem to them that they will
continue to exist as the True Infinite Self,
it *seems* to the human that
not only will the false self's existence cease
but that their existence will cease too.
That is why all humans are afraid
to go through the doorway to Manonasa.

There is a quote by Jan Frazier
that communicates this very clearly:

"Many spiritual seekers who say their wish is to awaken
don't actually want what they believe they do.
This becomes clear sometimes
at the approach to the brink of what feels like a void,
where the obliteration of the egoic self seems imminent.
With a shocked recognition of what is being asked,
the person will recoil.
The scale of the loss
– the dissolution of the familiar self –
is beyond what was bargained for."

This quote by Dr. David Hawkins helps to clarify also:

"The underpinnings of the ego
are its illusion that it is a separate self
and that the perceptions
which its positionality produces are real.
When these structures are transcended,
the ego brings up its last reserves.
These consist of the threat of death
or the threat of facing the total void of nothingness
or nonexistence.
When this arises, it becomes rapidly clear
that one is now forced to make a decision and choose."

"Into this gap in the flow of consciousness
there will arrive, beyond conscious recall,
the knowingness of the Sage, the Bodhisattva,
the Teacher, the Avatar,
the knowing-ness of the Enlightened beings of all times.
Instructions will be known:
'Hold back nothing;
completely surrender life itself to God.
Be willing to experience death.
Refuse the Void,
for it is merely another illusion of the ego
and has no reality.
Truth has no opposite.'
Faith in the teachings
of those who have realized the Truth is crucial.
They spring forth into awareness
and strengthen the willingness to surrender
and to experience the death
that is simultaneously the birth of the Self.
By invitation and surrender,
death becomes an experiential reality.
It can be fearful and intimidating for a brief moment.
It is not like the physical deaths
that occurred in previous incarnations
when one left the body with great relief.
This is actually the first and also the last time
that real death can be experienced.
Therefore, it need be gone through only one time ever.
With the courage of conviction
and the inspiration of the Self and its teachers,
one surrenders to the plunge.
For a few moments, the last great fear erupts and
one experiences what it really means to die completely
as the great door swings open to the Splendor,
beyond all comprehension.
The Presence reveals that the Infinite Splendor
is actually one's own Self."

"Innate is the knowingness that one's Reality
is beyond all lifetimes, beyond all universes,
total and complete."

Instead of the door to Manonasa,
if it makes it easier for you to understand,
you can call it **The Final Door**.

What M felt when the door to Manonasa appeared
was what all humans feel: FEAR.
What made M different from almost all humans
is that he did not let that fear stop him
from going through that door to Manonasa.
He went through that door and Manonasa occurred.

When Ramana Maharshi described
what happened just prior to his Manonasa
Ramana Maharshi said
"The fear of death drove my mind inward."
Yes Ramana Maharshi was afraid
at the doorway to Manonasa.
All humans are afraid at the doorway to Manonasa.
The difference between Ramana Maharshi
and almost all other humans is that
Ramana Maharshi went through the door to Manonasa
and allowed Manonasa to occur.

Here is how Ramana Maharshi described his Manonasa experience:

"So, on that day as I sat alone
there was nothing wrong with my health.
But a sudden and unmistakable fear of death seized me.
I felt I was going to die.
Why I should have felt so cannot be completely
explained by anything I felt in my body.
Nor could I explain it to myself then."

"I did not however trouble myself
to discover if the fear of death was well grounded.
I felt 'I was going to die,'
and at once set about thinking what I should do.
I did not care to consult doctors or elders
or even friends.
I felt I had to solve the problem myself then and there.
The shock of the fear of death made me at once
introspective, or 'introverted.'
I said to myself mentally,
i.e. without uttering the words
'Now death has come. What does it mean?
What is it that is dying? This body dies.'
I at once dramatized the scene of death.
I extended my limbs and held them rigid
as though rigor-mortis had set in.
I imitated a corpse
to lend an air of reality to my further investigation,
I held my breath and kept my mouth closed, pressing
the lips tightly together so that no sound might escape.
Let not the word 'I' or any other word be uttered!
'Well then,' I said to myself, 'this body is dead.
It will be carried stiff to the burning ground
and there burnt and reduced to ashes.
But with the death of this body, am 'I' dead?
Is the body 'I'?
The body is silent and inert.
But I feel the full force of my personality
and even the sound 'I' within myself,
apart from the body.
So 'I' am a spirit, a thing transcending the body.
The material body dies,
but the spirit transcending it
cannot be touched by death.
I am therefore the deathless spirit.'"

"All this was not a mere intellectual process,
but flashed before me vividly as living Truth,
something which I perceived immediately,
without any argument almost.
'I' was something very real,
the only real thing in that state,
and all the conscious activity that was
connected with my body was centered on that.
The 'I' or my 'Self' was holding the focus of my attention
by a powerful fascination from that time forwards.
Fear of death had vanished at once and forever.
Absorption in the Self has continued from that moment
right up to this time.
Other thoughts may come and go
like the various notes of a musician,
but the 'I' continues
like the basic or fundamental sruti note which
accompanies and blends with all other notes."

In the book *No Mind I Am the Self* you can read
about Saradamma's experience of both being at the door
to Manonasa and going through the door to Manonasa.
Saradamma's I-thought was so afraid
at the door to Manonasa,
the I-thought tried to escape
by breaking through her skull.
The difference between Saradamma
and almost all other humans is that in spite of the fear,
Saradamma went through the door to Manonasa
and allowed Manonasa to occur.

M went through the door to Manonasa
and allowed Manonasa to occur.
In January of 2004 the ego-mind came to its final end
and the ego-mind can never reappear in all of eternity.
All suffering and sorrow disappeared forever
and they can never reappear in all of eternity.

The body disappeared forever
and the body can never reappear in all of eternity.
The universe disappeared forever
and the universe can never reappear for all of eternity.
What remained when everything else disappeared is:
Absolutely Perfect
Infinite-Eternal-Awareness-Love-Bliss.

One of the many things that makes the book
The Seven Steps to Awakening so wonderful
is that you can see what Seven Sages
had to say on seven essential topics.
You do not have to rely on just Michael Langford's
account of these seven truths.
In the book *The Seven Steps to Awakening*
Seven Sages are in perfect agreement
about seven essential truths.

I like the book *The Seven Steps to Awakening*
better than the book *The Direct Means to Eternal Bliss.*
People are often surprised at that and they wonder
how can you like a book of quotes by others
better than the book you wrote?
The answer to that is when people read
The Direct Means to Eternal Bliss
they might think that is just one Sage's view.
However, when they read
The Seven Steps to Awakening
they can see that seven different Sages
were in agreement on seven Essential Truths
and seven different Sages
saw the same seven Essential Truths.

All seven of the subjects in the book
The Seven Steps to Awakening
are subjects that the ego-mind blocks out.
The ego-mind ignores those seven subjects.

The ego-mind does not remember those quotes
after it reads them.
Or the ego-mind changes the meaning of the quote
into something that is more acceptable to the ego-mind.

Therefore when M says
the body disappeared forever
and it can never return in all of eternity
and the universe disappeared forever
and it can never return in all of eternity
people think that is just Michael Langford's view.
However, there are many quotes in the book
The Seven Steps to Awakening
that teach that when the ego disappears
the world and body disappear and can never return.
Therefore by reading
The Seven Steps to Awakening
people can see it is not just Michael Langford's view.
Some of the step two quotes are on the subject
of the world, etc. being an illusion or a kind of dream.
Some of the quotes are on the subject of how
when the ego ends the body and universe disappear.
There are more than three hundred step two quotes.
All of those quotes are helpful for understanding.

What follows are some of the quotes by the Sages
from the book *The Seven Steps to Awakening*
that deal with the subjects of
the disappearance of the universe and the body, etc.
after Manonasa,
and that only the Self remains after Manonasa
and that the Self has never been aware of a body,
or a universe in all of eternity.
When people see a Sage's body
it is because they are still dreaming.
The Sage has no awareness of a body or a world.

230. What is Self's self-transformation as the world?
A twist of straw appearing as a snake?
Look hard you see no snake at all.
There was no transformation, no creation, none, no world at all.

238. O worldly folk who long for and run after
an endless series of unenduring things,
'tis wisdom true to seek and know That one thing
on knowing which
***all other things* will cease to be**.

247. Until the snake-illusion goes,
its ground, the real rope, will not be recognized.
Until the world of false phenomena **disappears**,
the Self, its ground, will not shine clear.

248. **Only when the world-illusion goes**
does the blissful light of Self arrive.
Life lived in this bright, blissful light
is our true, natural life.
Other ways of life are full of trouble and fear.

249. Is there a greater folly than the aching folly
of supposing that the Self, the I of pure awareness
which does not see this changing world at all,
is subject to some change?

534. **The false dream ends when we wake up**.
Even so, the ego dies when the sun, the true I, rises.
Ego's destruction by strong Self-inquiry
is what is known as Self-attainment.

543. Even as the ego does not die
unless the Self's glance falls on it,
the painful dream of this phenomenal world
will never **disappear**
unless the mind meets glorious death.

868. The deeds we do in dream
touch not our waking life,
but slip away when we awake.
Even so, our deeds done in this clouded ego-life
disappear and leave no trace when we wake up
in the divine white light of Self-awareness.

869. One whirls and turns, pines in sore pain
in this false dream world,
till at last the sleeper in his soft bed wakes up,
the bad dream ends,
one feels relieved, untouched,
free as the pure white screen.
Such freedom is Self-knowledge pure.

873. **Not an iota of the past**
can touch those who dwell unceasingly
in the firmament of Self-awareness
vast, boundless, frontierless and full.

881. Our real Being,
the sun **that can never see**
the darkness of illusion,
knows no trace of pain or suffering.
Misery is what one brings upon oneself
by fondly thinking that one is the body,
not the Self.

882. The goal, the Truth, is Self-awareness.
Reaching it is
annihilation of the painful illusion of birth.

887. Non-dual infinite Awareness
where **the error of seeing, hearing,**
knowing various objects has been destroyed,
this is the purest bliss serene.

898. The Sage enjoys as his own being
the bliss of all transcendent Being.
The error lies in these ignorant folk
seeing him as a body that suffers.

899. The Sage abiding in Self-being,
asleep and yet awake,
immersed in the still, deep immutable ocean
of bliss supreme,
will never lapse back into this ruinous world
and suffer.

1292. Those who diving deep within have found the Self
have nothing else to know.
And why?
Because they have gone themselves
beyond all forms
and are Awareness without form.

QUOTES BY ANNAMALAI SWAMI

267. Your real state is the Self,
and **in that Self there is no body and no mind**.

1455. You can only put your attention
on one thing at a time.
While it is on the mind or the body,
it cannot be on the Self.
Conversely, if you put attention on the Self
and become absorbed in it,
there will be no awareness of mind and body.

252. The eye of the Self, consciousness,
alone constitutes true seeing.
That eye **never perceives anything at all**.
It if be said that the eye perceives anything whatsoever,
then that eye too, like the thing it perceives,
is a mental creation.
It is not the true eye.

254. In the heart,
the Self that exists as the eye of grace,
none of the worlds truly exist.

258. The Self,
revealed as our true nature within the heart
through the power of Self-inquiry,
is none other than the peerless reality of the Supreme,
which alone remains
after this worldly illusion
has faded into nothingness.

261. If I am to affirm who I am,
my true nature,
I am the Self
that knows nothing of the fleshly body, life,
intelligence and mind,
that is free of all darkness,
the true 'I' that excels as pure consciousness.

271. **What do you know of me,
when even my talk with you
is in your world only**?

293. **He who knows the state
in which there is neither the world
nor the thought of it**,
he is the Supreme Teacher.

296. **You are neither the body nor in the body –
there is no such thing as body**.
You have grievously misunderstood yourself;
to understand rightly – investigate.

299. Without imagination **there is no world**.

306. Nothing dies.
**The body is just imagined.
There is no such thing**.

307. **There is no body, nor a world to contain it**;
there is only a mental condition,
a dream like state,
easy to dispel by questioning its reality.

302. Maharaj: **This body appears in your mind;
in my mind nothing is**.

Questioner: Do you mean to say
you are quite unconscious of having a body?

Maharaj: **On the contrary,
I am conscious of not having a body**.

Questioner: I see you smoking!

Maharaj: Exactly so.
You see me smoking.
Find out for yourself
how did you come to see me smoking,
and you will easily realize that **it is your**
'I-am-the-body' state of mind
that is responsible for this
'I-see-you-smoking' idea.

572. **I take my stand where no difference exists,**
where things are not,
nor the minds that create them.
There I am at home.

576. The realized man is egoless;
he has lost the capacity of
identifying himself with anything.
He is without location, placeless,
beyond space and time,
beyond the world.
Beyond words and thoughts is he.

601. **Even the idea of being man or woman,**
or even human should be discarded.

604. Keep on remembering:
I am neither the mind nor its ideas.
Do it patiently and with conviction
and you will surely come to the direct vision of yourself
as the source of being – knowing – loving,
eternal, all-embracing, all-pervading.
You are the infinite focused in a body.
Now you see the body only.
Try earnestly
and you will come to see the infinite only.

950. I was never born.
How can I grow old?
What I appear to be to you
exists only in your mind.
I am not concerned with it.

1332. To know the world you forget the Self –
to know the Self you forget the world.
What is world after all?
A collection of memories.
Cling to one thing, that matters,
hold on to 'I am' and let go all else.

1360. Now, go within,
into a state which
you may compare to a state of waking sleep,
in which **you are aware of yourself,**
but not of the world.
In that state you will know,
without the least trace of doubt,
that at the root of your being you are free and happy.

1363. **As long as you are engrossed in the world,**
you are unable to know yourself:
to know yourself,
turn your attention away from the world
and turn it within.

1367. The world appears to you so overwhelmingly real,
because you think of it all the time;
cease thinking of it and it will **dissolve** into thin mist.

1498. I used to sit for hours together,
with nothing but the 'I am' in my mind
and soon peace and joy
and a deep all-embracing love
became my normal state.
**In it all disappeared – myself, my Guru,
the life I lived, the world around me.**
Only peace remained and unfathomable silence.

QUOTES FROM THE YOGA VASISTHA

326. In truth,
this world does not arise from the absolute
nor does it merge in it.
The absolute **alone** exists now and for ever.

327. **All this is mere imagination or thought.
Even now nothing has ever been created;
the pure infinite space alone exists.**

328. Cosmic consciousness alone exists now and ever;
in it are no worlds, no created beings.

334. **There is no universe,
no distance, no barriers.**

339. When there is notion of creation,
the creation seems to be:
and when through self-effort,
there is understanding of non-creation,
there is no world.

341. When the mind entertains notions of objects,
there is agitation or movement in the mind;
and when there are no objects or ideas,
then there is no movement of thought in the mind.
When there is movement, the world appears to be;
when there is no movement,
there is cessation of world-appearance.

355. It is **only** in a state of ignorance
that the mind dreams of the world-appearance,
not when it is awake or enlightened.

356. Such indeed is the nature of this utter ignorance,
this delusion, and this world-process:
without real existence
there is this illusory notion of egotism.
This egotism does **not** exist in the infinite Self.
In the infinite Self there is no creator,
no creation, no worlds, no heaven, no humans,
no demons, no bodies, no elements, no time.

357. **There is no creation.**
The infinite has never abandoned its infinity.
THAT has never become this.

364. **The world is not seen**
in the supreme non-dual consciousness.

380. **There is no world in reality**.

393. I am the unborn
in whom **the world-appearance has vanished**.

394. It is **only** in the eyes of the ignorant
that even your form exists.

396. When one is firmly established in Self-knowledge,
which is infinite, unlimited and unconditioned,
then **the delusion or ignorance
that gave rise to the world-appearance
<u>comes to an end</u>**.

401. **The supreme Self
has no relationship with this world-appearance**.

402. The ignorant person accepts as real
whatever he sees in this world;
not so the wise one.
Even as a piece of wood
and the water in which it is reflected
have no real relationship,
the body and the Self have no real relationship.

404. There is no duality;
**there are no bodies
and therefore
there are no relationships among them**.

406. When the mind abandons
the movement of thought,
the appearance of the world-illusion <u>ceases</u>.

410. **Nothing has really become
physical or material**.

416. **You have nothing to do with birth, sorrow,
sin and delusion**.
Abandon all these notions and rest in the Self.

423. This world-illusion has arisen
because of the movement of thought in the mind;
when that ceases **the illusion will <u>cease</u> too**,
and the mind becomes no-mind.

434. There is but one consciousness
which is pure, indivisible,
the subtlest of the subtle, tranquil,
which is neither the world nor its activities.

439. On the awakening of the inner intelligence,
the world-perception ceases
and there arises psychological freedom
or non-attachment.
That is known as emancipation.

442. **It is only when the eyes
are blinded by ignorance
that one perceives the world of diversity**.

444. You are a knower.
Whether you know something or not,
remain free from doubt.
When you realize that you are the unborn,
infinite consciousness,
then all ignorance and foolishness cease
and **this world-appearance ceases**.

451. Creation, world, movement of consciousness, etc.
are mere words without substance.
When such ideas are abandoned,
the "world" and the "I" cease to be
and consciousness alone exists,
pure and immutable.
This unconditioned consciousness alone is,
**naught else is –
not even the nature of diverse objects here**.

456. In **their** mind, my body seems to be real;
but to **my** illumined intelligence,
their physical existence is unreal,
as it is to a sleeping person.

457. When one is fully established in the Self,
then **this world-appearance ceases**
like dream during deep sleep.

458. The **world appearance** arises in ignorance
and wisdom puts an **end** to it.

460. When what exists is realized as it is,
the world-appearance ceases.

463. **In the eyes of the wise man**
there is no world.

465. When wisdom is strengthened and confirmed,
and when the impurity of conditioning is washed away,
the holy one shines with an extraordinary radiance.
Both the inner notion and
the external perception of the world
cease for him.

468. **There is no such thing as earth or matter**.

470. **There is no such thing as the world**.

471. This body is but pure void,
it seems to exist on account of the mental conditioning.
When the latter ceases,
the body ceases to be seen or experienced,
just as the dream object is not experienced
on waking up.

472. **Neither the subtle body**
nor the gross body is seen
even in the waking state
when the mental conditioning ceases.

474. **You imagine that I have a body**.
It is on account of this notion existing in you
that I produce this sound known as speech.
You hear it
even as a sleeping person hears sounds
in his dream.

480. In the vision of the knowers of the truth,
there is nothing other than
the pure and infinite consciousness,
and **the objective universe**
is completely and totally non-existent.

486. **There is no death,**
and by the same token there is no birth either.

492. Just as the dream-mountain
is realized as pure void when the dreamer wakes up,
even so are
all these forms realized to be non-existent
when one is enlightened.

494. Only when it is realized that
there is no creation at all
does real Self-knowledge arise
which leads to liberation.
Such liberation is unending, infinite and unconditioned.

495. The objective universe is delusion or illusion;
it does not disappear **except** through
persistent practice.

499. **Something which is unreal**
does not arise in the real.

500. **There is no illusion in the infinite**.

501. **This illusion of world-appearance vanishes when one is awakened and enlightened. Then one realizes that it has never been, it is not and it will never be**.

502. **The unreal does not exist at all at any time**.

505. **Nothing, not even this body, has ever been created**.

507. What you have called the body **does not exist in the eyes of the Sage**.

508. **There is no "dream" in the infinite consciousness. There is neither a body nor a dream in it**.

511. It is **only** as long as you are **not** fully enlightened that you experience the apparent diversity.

630. It is the mind alone which is the cause of all objects of the world; the three worlds exist because of the mind-stuff; **when the mind vanishes, the worlds vanish too**.

632. **This diversity arises on account of mental modifications and it will cease when they cease**.

663. You will enjoy freedom when the mind **ceases** to be, **along with the world-illusion contained in it**.

675. If the ego-sense ceases to be, then **the illusory world-appearance does not germinate again** and all cravings come to an end.

698. As long as there is mind,
there is no cessation of sorrow.
When the mind ceases,
the world-appearance also ceases to be.
The mind is the seed for misery.

736. **The non-perception of objects**
and the non-arising of notions.
This should be experienced.

739. The supreme Self is in the supreme Self,
the infinite in the infinite, the peace in peace.
That is all there is,
neither "I" nor "the world" nor "the mind."

740. When the seed for the world-appearance
(which is the ego-sense)
has been **destroyed,**
the world-appearance goes with it.
Even as the mirror gets misted by moisture,
the Self is veiled by the unreal ego-sense.
This ego-sense gives rise
to all the rest of this world-appearance.
When it goes, then the Self shines by its own light,
even as the sun shines
when the veiling cloud is blown away.

745. If one is able to remove the ego-sense
by means of one's awakened intelligence,
he cleanses from his consciousness
the impurity known as world-appearance.

751. **When a dream-object perishes,**
nothing is lost:
when "the world" or "the I" is lost,
nothing is lost.

755. Matter and mind are identical;
and both are false.
You are deluded by this false appearance.
Self-knowledge will **dispel** this delusion.
Both Self-knowledge
and the cessation of world-appearance
are the characteristics of wisdom.

757. **To the wise there is neither ego-sense**
nor the world.

993. Whatever be the external appearance
of the liberated Sage,
his wisdom remains unchanged.
The difference is only in the eyes
of the ignorant spectator.

1020. To the enlightened vision,
only the infinite consciousness exists, naught else.
Do not become an ignorant man; become a Sage.
Destroy the mental conditioning
that gives rise to this world appearance.
Why do you, like an ignorant man,
consider this body as your self and feel miserable?

1095. The best of all states, O Sage,
is indeed the vision of the one infinite consciousness.
Even the contemplation of the Self
which is infinite consciousness
banishes sorrow, **terminates**
the long-dream vision of the world-appearance,
purifies the mind and the heart and dispels misfortunes.
That contemplation of the Self is devoid of mentation.

1377. **As long as the objective universe**
is perceived
one does not realize the Self.

1396. **This body can have no relationship whatsoever with the Self.**

1552. **The consciousness is freed from the object.** There is pure inner consciousness.

1559. **I abandoned all material**
and physical concepts
and held on to the vision of pure consciousness.

1560. **He who is enlightened**
sees not the diversity.

QUOTES BY ADI SANKARA

512. **Where has the world gone?**
Who has removed it,
or where has it disappeared to?
I saw it only just now, and now it is not there.

519. **I see not, nor hear,**
nor know aught of this world;
for I bear the mark of the Self,
whose form is being and bliss.

521. **The world no longer is,**
whether past, present, or to come,
after awakening to the supreme reality,
in the real Self, the Eternal, from all wavering free.

772. **So long as even a dreamlike awareness of yourself as an individual in the world remains, as a wise person persistently see to the removal of all ideas of additions to your true Self.**

775. The Sage who stands in the Eternal,
the Self of being, ever full,
of the secondless bliss of the Self,
has none of the hopes fitted to time and space that make for the formation of a body of skin, and flesh, subject to dissolution.

784. There is no unwisdom, except in the mind,
for the mind is unwisdom,
the cause of bondage to life;
when this is destroyed, all is destroyed;
when this dominates, the world dominates.

1210. I am free,
I am bodiless,
I am without sex and indestructible.
I am at peace;
I am infinite, without blemish and eternal.

1221. **I can neither see, hear or experience anything else there**,
as it is I who exist there by myself
with the characteristics of Being and Bliss.

1240. This knower of the Eternal,
ever bodiless,
things pleasant or painful touch not at all,
nor things fair or foul.

1247. Thus dwelling in the supreme Eternal,
through the real Self,
he stands alone and beholds naught else.
From the knowledge that I am the Eternal,
the accumulated works,
heaped up even through hundreds of myriads of ages,
melt away like the work of dream, on awaking.

1271. He who through the Self
dwells here in the secret place,
for him there is no coming forth again
to the world of form.

1426. This supreme Reality is non-dual
in the absence of any other reality beside itself.
In the state of knowledge of ultimate truth
there is nothing else.

MANONASA TEACHING STORIES

If the ego-mind allows a human to hear
what the Sages have been trying to communicate
to them about the fact that when Manonasa occurs
there is no longer any awareness of a body or a world
or a universe,
this brings up something that is very difficult
for a human to understand.
The human sees the body of a Sage
that has attained Manonasa
walking, talking, answering questions,
functioning normally, etc.
and the human wonders
if the Sage has no awareness or perception of a body
or a world
then how is it possible for the Sage to be talking,
walking, answering questions
and functioning normally?

Because this is so difficult for a human to
understand I have created many teaching stories
to communicate this understanding to the humans.
You can use another word for these stories if you prefer
such as illustrations, examples, metaphors, analogies,
etc. I prefer to call them Manonasa Teaching Stories.

The first teaching stories will come from the book *The Direct Means to Eternal Bliss.*

MANONASA TEACHING STORIES FROM THE BOOK *THE DIRECT MEANS TO ETERNAL BLISS*

Describing the final Reality as
Infinite-Eternal-Awareness-Love-Bliss
is the closest one can come in words.
In the final Reality, which is the only Reality,
there are **no humans, no animals, no planets, no stars, and no earth**.

The final Reality is
infinite awareness aware only of infinite awareness.
In all of eternity the final Reality has never been aware
of anything other than infinite-awareness-love-bliss.
Awareness-love-bliss are not three, it is one.
In all of eternity the final Reality, which is the true Self,
has **never been aware of a human, or a world or suffering of any kind**.
Humans, animals, earth, planets, stars, other realms,
entities, places, time, dimensions,
and that which almost every word in the dictionary
point towards is part of the ego dream.
When the ego comes to its final end,
the dream ends
and almost everything that the words in a dictionary
point towards **disappears.**

When the ego comes to its final end,
what remains is Infinite-Eternal-Awareness-Love-Bliss
and nothing ever reappears.
The planets, the stars, and almost everything that the
words in a dictionary point towards **never reappear**.

They were all part of the dream.
Upon awakening, **the dream disappears**.

The state humans consider to be their real life,
the state that occurs when they wake up from sleep
is a type of dream.
You could call it the waking-dream.
The type of dream that occurs when humans are
sleeping could be called the sleeping-dream.
There are many differences between the waking-dream
and the sleeping-dream.
For example there is a sense of continuity
in the waking-dream.
Humans wake up to the story where the story left off.
When the ego comes to its final end,
both the waking-dream and the sleeping-dream **end**.
**When the ego comes to its final end, there is
no longer the perception of a body or a world**.
That is not the same as saying the body dies.
If you go to sleep tonight and dream of flying camels,
when you wake up the flying camels did not die.
They just disappeared.

Suppose you have a friend named Joe.
Suppose that Joe is one of those rare
one in five hundred million humans
who succeeds in ending the ego illusion.
From the moment of ending the ego illusion
Joe no longer has any perception of a body or a world.
Yet from your perspective,
assuming you are one who is still dreaming
the human dream,
you will still perceive Joe's body functioning normally.
You will see Joe walking, talking, eating,
and going about daily activities.

An example to make this clearer is sleepwalking.
Sleepwalkers may get up from the bed,
go to the refrigerator, grab a glass of milk,
and drink the glass of milk all while remaining asleep.
The state of one who has ended the ego
is not identical with sleepwalking;
this example is provided because the human mind
tends to start with the assumption
that the Sage's body only being perceptible
to a third party onlooker
is something difficult to understand.

Here is yet another example.
There are two friends named Sally and Joe.
Joe is an astronaut.
Joe takes a ship to the moon.
Sally goes to sleep at night and has a dream.
In the dream Sally is talking to Joe.
But Joe is really on the moon.
Therefore, even though Sally sees Joe walking and
talking and sees Joe still living on earth in her dream,
Joe is not really on the earth.
This is also just an example
to make something more comprehensible
that humans find difficult to comprehend.
The awakened Sage has not gone to some other place.
In the case of an awakened Sage
the dream has ended that contained the place.
Both the sleeping-dream and the waking-dream
have ended for the awakened Sage.

Often when a human
wakes up from a sleeping-dream,
they have no memory of the sleeping-dream.
Or they have a memory only for a minute or so
upon awakening
and then they cannot remember their sleeping-dream.

The Sage who has awakened from both the
sleeping-dream and the waking-dream
has no memory of ever having been human.
Yet to one still dreaming it will **appear**
that the Sage is still carrying on normal physical life.
To one still dreaming the Sage will **appear**
to be talking, eating, answering questions, etc.
**The one still dreaming creates a waking-dream
that includes the appearance of the body
of the awakened Sage**.

When you go to sleep at night
and have a sleeping-dream
all that appears in your sleeping-dream
is just your consciousness.
All the people you communicate with
and all the places
are really just your own consciousness.
They are not real.
They are your consciousness appearing as people,
places, events and things.
Therefore what they really are is one consciousness
that has the ability to appear as everything in the dream.

The example just given
applies to the waking-dream also.
Everything you perceive in the waking-dream,
which is what humans mistakenly call real life,
is one consciousness that has the ability to appear
as everything including almost everything
that the words in the dictionary point towards.
That one consciousness appears
as both things and actions.

There is a description that is much closer to the Truth of the final Reality:

The final Reality <u>never</u> appears
as the earth, humans or almost anything
that the words in the dictionary point towards.
The final Reality always remains as it is
and there has <u>never</u> been a human, planet
or almost anything the words in a dictionary
point towards in the final Reality.

One can use the example of a movie theatre.
In some places this may be called cinema.
The light inside the light bulb in the projector
represents the final Reality
or in other words the True Self.
The film represents thoughts, feelings, emotions,
the body, the five senses, etc.
On the screen a world is seen.
However, inside the light which is inside the projector
there is no world, no movie, no people etc.

All of what is described here can be known in direct experience by bringing the ego to its final end.

The difference between
the deep dreamless sleep state and the final Reality
is that in the deep dreamless sleep state
there appears to be unconsciousness.
In the final Reality there is awareness
that never changes and is always there.

When you wake up from the sleeping-dream,
where did the world and people you dreamed about go?
They did not go anywhere.
They were never really there
even while you were dreaming.

So it is when you wake up
from the human waking-dream.
The planets, people, animals, plants, stars, etc.
were never really there.
They seemed real while you were dreaming them
in the waking-dream,
just like what you experience in the sleeping-dream
seems real while you are dreaming it.
When you wake up from the waking-dream,
which happens when the ego comes to its final end,
the planets, people, animals, plants, stars, etc.
disappear,
similar to how whatever you dream
in the sleeping-dream disappears upon your waking up.

Imagine an ocean of consciousness.
Instead of an ocean of water,
this is an ocean of consciousness.
Almost all of the waves on this ocean of consciousness
have developed the habit of never looking down.
They only look out horizontally.
Because they only look out horizontally
all they see are what appears to be
billions of separate waves.
They assume that there is no ocean,
only separate waves.
One day one of these waves has the courage
to dive deep down within itself and discovers the ocean.
This wave discovers that
there is no line that separates it from the ocean.
This wave discovers that there are no waves,
there is only the ocean.
Wave is a concept created by imagining there is a
bottom line that separates the wave from the ocean.
There are no waves, there is only the ocean.
This can be known in direct experience.

AN EMAIL TO A STUDENT

One of my students had learned very well
that everything that people see
in the behavior of the awakened Sage's body
is their dream, their projection,
or in other words the dream or projection
of the one doing the observing.
However, she temporarily forgot that
and I sent her this email as a clarification:

So you are talking about the difference
in perspective between Nisargadatta saying
he is not aware of the body or the world
and other people seeing him talking, etc..
And as you know Nisargadatta had
so many different ways of stating that same theme.
You mentioned: Ramana Maharshi being concerned
in the kitchen about how vegetables were cut,
Nisargadatta appearing to be sitting there smoking
and Michael Langford publishing books.
How can they do all of that
and yet not be aware of the world?
I don't know how that can be.

There is a common error in thinking that occurs.
Here is an attempt to explain it
in a way that I have not tried before.
The error is confusing the levels.
Ramana Maharshi is the name of a body.
That body is just as aware of the world as you are.
Nisargadatta is the name of a body.
That body is just as aware of the world as you are.
Michael Langford is the name of a body.
That body is just as aware of the world as you are.

It is the Self that is not aware of the body
or the world or the universe.
It is the Self that has no body, no world and no universe.
The Self has no name.
The name Nisargadatta Maharaj,
the name Ramana Maharshi,
the name Michael Langford does not exist in the Self.

The bodies called Nisargadatta Maharaj,
Ramana Maharshi, Michael Langford
are just as much of an illusion as your body.
So a question might arise
is there any difference then between the body of a Sage
and the body of one in whom
the ego illusion has not yet ended?
Yes there is a difference:
inside that illusory appearance of the Sage's body
there is no ego illusion.
Therefore when the body of the Sage speaks
it can report accurately about the Self.
An example that you and I are both fond of using
is the prism and the sun.
Inside your body is the mind illusion (the prism)
therefore you cannot see the Self (the sun) clearly.
Inside the Sage's body is no mind illusion (no prism)
therefore the Sage can see the Self (the sun) clearly.
The word Sage refers to a body.
That body is an illusion just as your body is an illusion.

A question might arise
what happened to the individual ego consciousness
called Venkataraman
(Ramana Maharshi's name at birth)
when Venkataraman's mind died?

Here is an example to answer that question:
Suppose you go to the last ten feet of a river
just before it goes into the ocean.
You put a stone on the spot
where the river meets the ocean.
Then you measure ten feet from that stone up river
and put another stone.
So now you have marked off the last ten feet of the river
before it merges into the ocean.
Let's say that it will take five minutes for the water
in that river that is between those two stones
to go into the ocean.
Every five minutes let us give the name of that particular
water in that particular section a new name.

Let's suppose you have one of those watches
that you click and it starts the clock.
So you give the particular water
that is currently in that ten feet section a name,
say Venkataraman for example.
At the same time as you give it a name
you click your stop watch.
After five minutes all of the water
that was in that particular ten foot section
is now in the ocean.

Now suppose that the water in both the river
and the ocean is actually consciousness.
Now that the particular water-consciousness
that was in that last ten foot section at that time
is in the ocean of consciousness,
and it is only aware of the ocean of consciousness.
It is not aware of the river of consciousness.
However, everyone looking on will say
"The river is still there, I see it".
Of course everyone will still see the river.
The river is still there.

However, that particular water-consciousness
that was in that particular section five minutes ago
is now the ocean of consciousness.
You can not redirect that particular water
back out of the ocean now that it is in the ocean.
There is only the ocean of consciousness.
People will still see a river.
However, it is different water-consciousness
even though it looks like the exact same river
to the onlooker.

At this point the river represents
the body of the Sage.
The movement of the river represents
the apparent actions of the Sages.
After the five minutes have passed
the onlooker will still see a river
that looks just as it looked before.
After the ego illusion ends people will see
the Sage's body looking just as it looked before.
However, the individual mind consciousness
that was there before is no longer there
and is no longer aware of a body.
The onlooker after the five minutes has passed
will still see the river water moving.
The onlooker will still see the Sage's body
engaged in various activities.
However,
the individual mind consciousness has disappeared
and is no longer aware of the body's activities.
The onlooker will assume that it is the same river.
However the five minutes has passed
and that particular ten foot section of water
is now only the ocean of consciousness.
It is no longer a river.

The Sage's body may look the same
when it is cutting vegetables before the ego illusion ends
and after the ego illusion ends.
However,
the consciousness that lived in that body before
does not live in that body anymore.
That river has merged into the ocean.

The question may arise why does not
the illusory body appearance end when the mind ends?
The answer is: end for whom?
The appearance of a body and a world
has completely ended
for the individual mind consciousness
when that individual mind consciousness ends
in Manonasa.
The ocean remains as it has always remained,
unchanged.
Why does the illusory body of the Sage
appear to those still dreaming?
Because they are still dreaming.

When the illusory body
called Nisargadatta Maharaj
says I am not aware of the body or the world
he is referring to the Self.
Then someone thinks
I don't see how he can talk
and yet not be aware of the world.
This is the error, this is the mixing of the levels.
Nisargadatta did not say that the body
is not aware of the world.
Nisargadatta did not say that the body now talking
is not aware of the world.
He said I am not aware of the body and the world.
The illusory body called Nisargadatta
is as aware of the world as you are.

Since Nisargadatta is the name of a body,
the illusion called Nisargadatta
is as aware of the world as you are.
It is the Self that is not aware of the world or the body.

Nisargadatta had a different name at birth
before they started calling him Nisargadatta Maharaj.
I don't remember the name
but let's just use a name for an example: devadatta.
The individual consciousness mind called devadatta
came to an end.
From that moment onwards
that individual consciousness mind
is no longer aware of the world or the body.
Just like the river between the stones
in the above example.

As you know
one will never get this fully from the words.
However,
one does not need to keep making the same mistake
in thinking over and over by confusing the levels.
As a temporary exercise it can be helpful
when looking at a Nisargadatta quote
to say to yourself Nisargadatta's illusory body said this.
Nisargadatta is an illusory name
given to an illusory body.
When Nisargadatta says I am not aware of the world
or the body he means
the Self is not aware of the world or the body.
Nisargadatta is aware of the world and the body.
When Nisargadatta is speaking always remember
it is an illusory body that is speaking.
When Nisargadatta says I am not aware of the body
or the world he does not mean that the one speaking
to you now is not aware of the body or the world.

The Self that is not aware of the body or the world
has never spoken a word in all of eternity
and it has never had a thought in all of eternity.

A FEW MORE MANONASA TEACHING STORIES

THE PROJECTOR

Nisargadatta says he has no body,
yet a human still dreaming sees him talking etc.
The same is true
for all those who have attained Manonasa.
One still dreaming the human dream will see a body
that appears to be functioning normally,
walking, talking, writing, eating, etc.

So here is yet another way to explain this.
Let us suppose that there was a movie theater screen
that was alive.
Movie theater screens are not alive normally.
This is a special movie screen that is fully conscious.

You, the human still dreaming,
are the projectionist in the projection booth.
You therefore, are operating the projector.
You are the one selecting the film.
You are the one who turns the projector on
and starts it running.
You turn on the projector
and now the screen that was just a blank white screen
before has a movie projected on to it.

This special conscious movie screen
has a special ability.
It can speak through one of the characters
you have projected onto the screen.

One of the characters that you are projecting
onto the screen is called Mr. Self Realized Sage.
This special conscious movie screen
has the ability to speak through Mr. Self Realized Sage.

Mr. Self Realized Sage says I have no body.
The projectionist watching the movie says
of course you have a body
I just watched your body say I have no body.
I see your body moving, walking, talking,
and responding to my questions.

Mr. Self Realized Sage says
what you are seeing is the movie
you are projecting onto the Screen.
I am the Screen
and the reason you see a body walking,
talking, etc. is because you are projecting a body
that walks, and talks, etc. unto the screen.

Of course another way to say all this
is that you are dreaming a dream.
You see a body called Mr. Self Realized Sage
in your dream.
It is **your** dream,
it is **not** Mr. Self Realized Sage's dream.

MR. WHITE SUIT

Let us suppose that before you go to sleep tonight
you put a portable computing device on your bed
next to your ear.
You begin dreaming of a man in a white suit.
The device on your bed says to you,
I am formless, nameless, timeless and I have no body.
In your dream you dream that it is the man
you are dreaming of in the white suit
that is saying all that to you.

You say to the man in the white suit
of course you have a body,
I just saw and heard your body speak to me.
You dream the man in the white suit is telling you
"You are only dreaming of a man in a white suit,
I am really a device next to your ear."
However, since you are still dreaming
that everything is being said by the man in the white suit
you just cannot believe a man in a white suit
is not talking to you
and that it is only because you are dreaming
that you are seeing a man in a white suit.

So it is with the Sages.
You dream a Sage has a body and is talking to you.
However, the Sage is really the Self and has no body.

THE PRISM EYEGLASSES

Suppose that a beam of white light was conscious and had the ability to talk.

Suppose there were prism eyeglasses.
I don't know if prism eyeglasses exist or not
however they certainly could be made.
By prism eyeglasses I mean eyeglasses
that could do just what a prism does.
It turns white light into lights of many different colors.

So in this example we will suppose
that a person is wearing prism eyeglasses.
Or the person is holding a prism up to his eyes
so that what he sees now is only that
which is post prism, not pre prism.
Pre prism is the white beam of light.
Post prism is a bunch of colored lights.

The person wearing the glasses
has a conversation with the beam of white light.
The person says oh you have so many beautiful colors.
The white light says I have no colors.
I am only a beam of white light.
The person says what you are telling me is absurd.
I can see all your different colors quite clearly.

It is the same for those who see a Sage walking, talking, eating, etc.
Walking, talking, eating, etc.
are like those post prism colors.
The Sage is the Self and he has no body.
You are wearing prism glasses
and you see the Sage with a body
walking, talking, eating, etc.
Those prism glasses are called the human dream.

A TRIBUTE TO YOGI KANNA

I first began sharing the
Awareness Watching Awareness discovery
on the internet.
The first edition of the Eternal Bliss book
was an internet version.
Later there was a printed version.

Yogi Kanna read the Eternal Bliss book
in its first internet version.
From the first time he read the Bliss book
he knew I was his primary teacher.
He always treated me as his primary teacher
and he always communicated with me
in a way that made it clear he was my student
and I was his primary teacher.
He had some interest in other teachings
however his main focus was the Eternal Bliss book.

I usually do not reply to emails from people,
however from the time Yogi Kanna first emailed me
until his body passed away more than 11 years later
in October of 2015
I answered almost every email that Yogi Kanna sent me.

I never criticized Yogi Kanna.
That is the way I work with my core students.
I do not criticize them.
The reason I do not criticize them is because the
unconditional love and encouragement that I give them
is far more valuable than any criticism.

When in March of 2014 Yogi Kanna realized
that I had been giving him unconditional love and
encouragement with no criticism for more than 10 years
it had a profound effect on him.

In March of 2014 Yogi Kanna sent me an email
that described him expanding into infinite space
and being afraid and backing out.
I knew that he had been at the doorway to Manonasa.
He was a bit disappointed at having backed out.
I sent him a 38 minute recording,
that covered many topics.
One of those topics was not to criticize himself
too harshly for backing out or for having fear
because every human has fear
at the doorway to Manonasa
and almost all humans back out.

A few hours before his body passed away in October of 2015 Yogi Kanna sent me this email:

Dear Michael,

Thank you so much for your well wishes for Good health and your encouraging email along with spiritual inputs. It means a lot to me.

Also thanks so much for sharing the story of the father of your body. It's an amazing story.

I wouldn't mind losing this bodily life at all, actually the sooner the better as I'd be relieving myself and my parents of a huge burden. But those around me strongly advise me not to bring the thought of death ever, as they feel the will to live is the most important factor in healing. So I'll just focus repeating the sentence in my mind "I am not this body, I am infinite consciousness." And accept whatever happens to the body with gratitude.

Thank you for everything you've done for this world and for me. If the bodily life ends, I hope in the next life, I'm able to discover your direct path teachings very soon and able to dedicate my life to Manonasa.

If the body gets better, I'll communicate again in a few weeks or months.

Thank you for everything from the depth of my heart.

With great love and gratitude,
Kannan

Yogi Kanna sent me that email a few hours before his bodily life ended.

When I say that people will be studying my Teachings for thousands of years to come Yogi Kanna's statement a few hours before his body's death may help you to understand that and why it is so important to protect these Teachings:

"*Thank you for everything you've done for this world and for me.*
If the bodily life ends,
I hope in the next life I'm able to discover
your direct path teachings very soon
and able to dedicate my life to Manonasa."

Yogi Kanna had been my student for more than 11 years.
He knew from his experience
the value of these Teachings.
In his next life
he wished to discover these Teachings again.
That was his wish
a few hours before his bodily life came to an end.

I miss Yogi Kanna.
My core group of students also miss Yogi Kanna.
Yogi Kanna wrote two books:
Nirvana: Absolute Freedom and *Return to Love.*
His website is www.yogikanna.com
You can put his name in youtube
and a few videos will come up.

Yogi Kanna was a great spiritual student.
Yogi Kanna arrived at the doorway to Manonasa
which is something that
less than one in ten million humans does.

I am fortunate to have had
such an excellent spiritual student
as Yogi Kanna was.

Most people tend to think
that when an Awakened Sage is talking to a student
that everything the Sage says
is a part of his or her teaching
and therefore helpful for awakening.
This is not true as the following saying
of Sri Ramana Maharshi illustrates:

**"The Sage's pure mind
which beholds as a mere witness
the whole world is like a mirror
which reflects the foolish thoughts
of those who come before him.
And these thoughts are then *mistaken* to be his."**

In *The Seven Steps to Awakening*
that is quote number 34.
Thousands of pages of quotes have been printed
because of the **mistaken** view that
everything a Sage says is a part of his or her teachings.
Seven Steps quote number 34
corrects that mistaken view.
**If you understand the full significance
of that Ramana Maharshi quote
it can completely change your approach
to studying spiritual teachings.
It changes everything.**
Here is an example:
Some editions of *Talks with Sri Ramana Maharshi*
have 724 pages.
The book *How to Practice Self Inquiry*
has almost everything Ramana Maharshi said
about how to practice Self inquiry
from the book *Talks with Sri Ramana Maharshi.*
The book How to Practice Self Inquiry is only 102 pages!

In the book *Talks with Sri Ramana Maharshi*
there are more than 500 pages
that fall into one of these categories:
1. Reflections of the foolish thoughts
of those who came before him.
2. Distractions and Detours.

The impostor self wants to read those reflections
of the foolish thoughts of those who came before him.
The impostor self wants to read those distractions
and detours.
The impostor self wants to see great spiritual value
in those reflections of the foolish thoughts
of those who came before him.
The impostor self wants to see great spiritual value
in those distractions and detours.
Sri Ramana Maharshi gave everyone
a **completely new way to view** what people believe
are a Sage's spiritual teachings in quote 34 on page 215.
The impostor self in most people
does not want to put that quote 34 into practice
or to see its implications.
There is a level of intensity
the extremely intense desire for liberation can reach
that allows the student to see which teachings
are a reflection of the foolish thoughts of the student,
which teachings are distractions and detours,
nothing more,
and which teachings are the teachings of the Sage.

Here is a quote by Ramana Maharshi
from the book *Talks with Sri Ramana Maharshi*:

"Vichara Sagara is full of logic and technical terms.
Can these ponderous volumes serve any real purpose?
However, some people read them and seek Sages
only to see if they can meet their questions.
To read them, to discover new doubts and to solve them,
is a source of pleasure to them.
Knowing it to be a sheer waste,
the Sages do not encourage such people.
Encourage them once and there will be no end.
Only the inquiry into the Self can be of use.
Those familiar with logic,
Vritti Prabhakara, Vichara Sagara or Sutra Bhashya,
or similar large works,
cannot relish small works like *Truth Revealed*
dealing only with the Self and that pointedly too,
because they have accumulated vasanas
(latent tendencies or habits).
Only those whose minds are less muddy,
or are pure
can relish small and purposeful works."

That Ramana Maharshi quote shows the
great value of the book *How to Practice Self Inquiry*
that is only 102 pages
instead of the 724 pages in the book Talks
from which the quotes were gathered.
That quote also shows the great value of the book
The Seven Steps to Awakening
that has 240 pages in the first edition
or 195 pages in the second edition
instead of the eight books
from which the quotes were drawn
which total 2228 pages.
Two thousand two hundred twenty eight pages!

The Ramana Maharshi quotes on pages 215 & 217
warn against seeking more and more words
in spiritual teachings.
The reasons for those warnings
are very different in those two quotes.
The Step One quotes in the book
The Seven Steps to Awakening
warn against seeking more and more words, ideas
and concepts.
Thought can find a rationalization, justification, reason
or excuse for doing anything it wants to do
including reading thousands of pages of teachings
that are mostly a reflection of the foolish thoughts
of the student.
The same mind then judges its reasons
as good valid reasons.

Consider this quote by Lao Tzu from the Hua Hu Ching:

"**Not all spiritual paths
lead to the Harmonious Oneness.
Indeed, most are distractions and detours,
nothing more**."

Just three quotes,
the two Ramana Maharshi quotes on pages 215 & 217
and the Lao Tzu quote above
**can completely change your view
of spiritual teachings**.
Regarding the Lao Tzu quote
if you ever present the quote to someone
who has never seen it before,
most people have the same thought.
They think well maybe those spiritual paths
do not lead to the Harmonious Oneness
but maybe they are a necessary step
in the person's spiritual journey.

All humans are liars.
All humans lie to themselves every day.
It is as though Lao Tzu anticipated the lie to come
so he put in his quote the words "nothing more."
If those paths were a necessary step
in a person's spiritual journey
they would be something more than
a distraction or detour.
Lao Tzu said "nothing more."
When the extremely intense desire for liberation arises
a human can finally see that most spiritual paths and
teachings are distractions and detours, nothing more.

The book *How to Practice Self Inquiry*
gives the essence in 102 pages
without having to go through 724 pages
of the book Talks to try to find the teachings
that are not distractions and detours.

Now lets come back to the subject of the book
The Seven Steps to Awakening.
What the book *How to Practice Self Inquiry*
does for the book Talks,
the book *The Seven Steps to Awakening*
does for the eight books it draws its quotes from.
The Seven Steps to Awakening does not include quotes
that were a reflection of the foolish thoughts
of the questioner.
The Seven Steps to Awakening does not include quotes
that are distractions and detours.
Look at the power of that!
The Seven Steps to Awakening is a new spiritual path.

The quotes in the book
The Seven Steps to Awakening were typed
exactly as they were in the eight books
the quotes were gathered from.
Not one word was changed.
Not one word was added.
Therefore you might wonder how can
The Seven Steps to Awakening
be called a new spiritual path?
Read this over many times and reflect on it
and you may see the great power and value of
The Seven Steps to Awakening
and why it is a new spiritual path.
Reflect on the Ramana Maharshi quotes on pages
215 & 217 again and you will see why reading quotes in
The Seven Steps to Awakening in which
the reflections of the foolish thoughts of the student,
and distractions and detours have not been included
is not the same as reading 1. The Yoga Vasistha.
2. I Am That. 3. Annamalai Swami Final Talks.
4. The Path of Sri Ramana, Part One.
5. Sri Guru Ramana Prasadam.
6. The Garland of Guru's Sayings.
7. Charles Johnston's English translation of
The Crest Jewel of Wisdom.
8. John Richard's English translation of
The Crest Jewel of Wisdom.

One of the most significant aspects
of the book *The Seven Steps to Awakening*
is that the quotes have been gathered together
on seven essential teachings (the steps)
one subject at a time.
The impostor self does not like to focus on one subject.
It likes to go from one subject to the next.
That is one way the impostor self
preserves its imaginary self.

By having quotes by Seven Sages on one subject
before going unto the next subject
the mind has a chance to really absorb that teaching,
that lesson, that step, that subject.
By having seven Sages teach on one subject
you can see it was not just one Sage's teaching.
Seven different styles of communication
on a single subject has a much better chance of
penetrating the human mind's
thousands of layers of self deception.

There are a huge number of contradictions
in the original source books.
Most of the contradictions were not included in
The Seven Steps to Awakening.
Imagine a map that tells you to take a right turn
and the next day says never take a right turn.
That would be a bad map.
The contradictions being referred to here
are not between the books.
Within each of the eight books there are contradictions.
Back to the example of a map,
if you wanted the most direct route to get from
point A to point B then a map with hundreds of
distractions and detours would not be of much use.

This is how *The Seven Steps to Awakening* book was created: I read the eight source books one at a time. I was looking for quotes that met this criteria:

No distractions or detours.
Essential quotes
for the Direct Path of Awareness.
No quotes that were the reflection of
the foolish thoughts of the student.
Only the quotes that would lead towards
the end of illusion
and not towards more illusion.
In other words the most helpful quotes
for someone
who really wanted to end the illusion
and not just read about it.
Quotes for those who wanted
the Direct Experience
and not just the theory.
Quotes for those who wanted Realization
and Freedom and not just more words.

After circling the quotes I wondered
what category would this quote fall under?
Then I wrote the category (step) in the margin
of the book so I would know where to place it later.
I did not start with seven categories
and then look for quotes to fit them.
I did not start with any category.
I just circled quotes that met the criteria listed above
and then wondered what category those quotes would
fall under and then wrote the category in the margin.
That is how the seven categories arose.
I called them steps because steps are something you put
into practice. Those seven steps are seven essential
truths. I arranged those steps in the order
that would be most helpful.

For example,
the Step One quotes show how to use the quotes
as practice instructions
and how not to take the quotes intellectually
or theoretically.
The reason that step is first
is because if one does take the quotes in a way
that just makes them into a thought journey,
then all the other steps would not be effective.

The reason for not including a quote
is as important as the reason for including a quote.
People who read the source materials
will love the quotes that were excluded,
unless their desire for liberation is strong.
They will imagine great spiritual value
in the quotes that were not included.
Such is the tricky nature of the impostor self.
They will see great spiritual value in what
Ramana Maharshi says are the reflection of
the foolish thoughts of those who come before the Sage.
They will see great value in more words
(as the quote from the book Talks warns against)
as though 1574 quotes were not enough,
as though 195 or 240 pages were not enough
and one needed to go to the source books
for more words.

If some of you who have read the book
The Seven Steps to Awakening have noticed a power
or a unity or a transmission or a revelation that
is different from any other book you have read before,
reading this section of this autobiography about
The Seven Steps to Awakening may help you to
understand why.

The book *The Seven Steps to Awakening*
has the undiluted concentrated focus
of the essential essence of Seven Sages Teaching.
Seven Sages of the Direct Path of Awareness.
Seven Sages who succeeded
in bringing the impostor self
and all illusion and suffering to its final end.
Seven Sages who attained Manonasa.

Note on the statement
that not one word was changed:
in quote 1405 there was a typo in the first edition.
The word "too" should have been typed as the word "to."
That has been corrected in the second edition.

If just one individual
is writing a spiritual teaching
you may wonder if it is just that individual
or have others seen the same thing,
especially in a teaching like these
New Unique Direct Path to Manonasa teachings.
One of the many beauties of the book
The Seven Steps to Awakening
is that Seven different Sages who attained Manonasa
are quoted.
Therefore it was **not** just one individual
who saw these Truths.

This is some indication of what subjects are covered in each step of *The Seven Steps to Awakening:*

The Step One quotes are about not taking the teachings intellectually or wasting time arguing about or discussing the teachings.

The Step Two quotes are about
the fact that the world
and everything else perceived by humans
is a dreamlike illusion.

Manonasa is about the end of the ego-mind.
The Step Three quotes are about the ego-mind.

The Step Four quotes are about
the Desire for Liberation.

If you are interested in the bliss of the Self
many of the Step Five quotes are on that topic.
The Step Five quotes are also for the purpose of
motivating and encouraging you.

The Step Six quotes are about
Turning your Attention inward.

If you are interested in the fact
that the Self is Awareness,
most of the Step Seven quotes are on that topic.
The Step Seven quotes also describe
the most rapid and direct practice
for attaining Manonasa.

Many times in this autobiography
it has been repeated that the cause for Manonasa
in those very rare beings who attain Manonasa
is **not** grace, magic, some deity, luck, destiny or fate.
The cause for Manonasa is the awakening of
the extremely intense desire for Manonasa
and dropping all of your unnecessary activities
and using all of the free time thus created to practice
the most direct and rapid means to Manonasa.

What follows is an illustration to show how
thinking that the cause of Manonasa, Nirvana,
Self-Realization etc. is grace, magic, some deity, luck
or fate is a trick created by the ego to preserve the ego.

TWO MEN AND THE WELL

There was a man named Scared
who was very afraid of water.
Scared wanted to dig a well.
However, this set up a conflict because on the one hand
Scared wanted to dig a well to find water,
on the other hand Scared was very afraid of water.
Scared began discussing digging a well
with many people.
Discussing was a way of avoiding digging the well.
Thus it was Scared's fear of finding water that led him
to spend his time discussing instead of digging.

Almost all of the people
Scared discussed digging a well with
were also very afraid of water
and therefore they had developed
many ways of avoiding digging a well.
They were pretending to be discussing how to find water
when what they were really doing
is helping each other to avoid finding water.

One of the people told Scared
you do not need to dig a well to have water
for your property.
Grace will give you the water.
Due to the fact that Scared was afraid of water,
Scared was very open and receptive to this idea
that grace would provide the water
and that Scared did not need to dig a well.
Ten years passed as Scared waited for Grace
to provide the water.
Grace did **not** provide the water.

Scared was having a conversation
with someone else who told him
that the best way to dig a well is to use magic.
Because Scared was very afraid of water,
Scared was receptive to this idea
that he did not need to dig a well
because magic would dig the well for him.
Ten more years went by
while Scared learned all about magic
and tried to use magic to bring water to his property.
Magic did **not** provide the water.

Scared talked to another person who told Scared
you do not need to dig a well.
What you need is good luck
and a well will spontaneously appear on your property.
Scared was very receptive to this idea
because Scared was afraid of water.
Scared spent the next ten years reading books
about how to bring good luck.
Luck did **not** make a well appear on Scared's property.

Scared was talking to another person
who told him that there is nothing you can do
about either digging a well or not digging a well.
Your Karma will determine that.
Your fate or destiny will determine that.
If it is your destiny it will happen.
If it is not your destiny it will not happen.
Scared was very receptive to this idea
because Scared was afraid of water.
Scared had heard that his Karma could be improved
by doing good deeds.
Scared spent the next ten years doing good deeds.
Destiny did **not** dig a well for Scared.

Scared was talking to another person
who told him you do not need to dig a well.
What you need to do is
to pray to the great god Stinkyboodlenoodle.
The great god Stinky will provide the well for you.
Scared was very receptive to this idea
because scared was afraid of water.
Scared spent the next ten years
praying to the great god Stinky.
Stinky did **not** provide a well for Scared.
Fifty years had passed
and there was still **no** well on Scared's property.
Scared's body suddenly died.

There was another man named Honest.
Honest had the idea to dig a well on his property.
Honest began digging.
Honest never had any discussions with people
about digging
because Honest did not have time for discussions since
Honest was using all of his free time to dig that well.
Honest had dropped all of his unnecessary activities
to create more time for digging his well.
Honest succeeded and had a beautiful well
that provided him with water forever.

The book *The Importance of Practice & Effort*
is a collection of quotes by Seven Sages
all of whom attained Manonasa.
In the book *The Importance of Practice & Effort*
those Seven Sages explain why it is **not** grace, magic,
some deity, destiny or fate
that is the cause of Manonasa.
It is practice that is the cause of Manonasa.

The following five books combined
create a new spiritual path
that has no distractions or detours
and in which
the reflections of the foolish thoughts of the questioner
have not been included.

THESE FIVE BOOKS ARE THE FOUNDATION OF A **NEW UNIQUE** DIRECT PATH TO MANONASA:

1. *The Seven Steps to Awakening.*

2. *The Direct Means to Eternal Bliss.*

3. *How To Practice the Teachings.*

4. *Manonasa: A Spiritual Autobiography.*

5. *Experience Your Perfect Soul.*

Because **a specific type of**
Self-Awareness practice
has been the most successful method in human history
for producing the most humans
who have attained Manonasa
I am continuing to teach
a specific type of Self-Awareness practice,
sometimes using my words
and sometimes using the words of
the Seven Sages in the book
The Seven Steps to Awakening.

However, only one out of every
five hundred million humans attains Manonasa.
Therefore I am always interested in ways
to make the Self-awareness practice more effective.

I have now had 12 years Teaching experience
since the Manonasa occurred in January of 2004.
Therefore I have had an opportunity
to see what is effective and what is not effective
or in other words to see what succeeds
and what does not succeed.

One hour of Self-Awareness practice
from the heart
produces more progress towards Manonasa
than one thousand hours of
Self-Awareness practice from the head.

Even after many years of practice
most people who practice Self-Awareness
are still practicing from the head.

Listening to certain spiritual music
can move someone out of their head
and towards their heart.
My current recommendation
is that people listen to one or two songs
that touch their heart
before every Self-Awareness practice session.

I have created four spiritual music video playlists
on youtube
designed to move people from their head to their heart.

I have noticed that people
who do not read one of the five books in this
New Unique Direct Path to Manonasa
every day eventually give up their practice.
Sometimes after just a few weeks or months.
Sometimes after a few years.
Then they go on to some other teaching.

Therefore I have changed my recommendation.
For most of the years I recommended
people drop all of their unnecessary activities
and use all of the free time thus created
to practice Self-Awareness.

I have changed that recommendation to the following:

Drop all of your unnecessary activities
and use ½ of the free time thus created
to practice Self-Awareness
and use the other ½ of the free time thus created
to reread each of the five books from this
New Unique Direct Path to Manonasa
hundreds of times
over, and over, and over again.

Reading one of those five books every day serves many purposes:

1. The ego-mind is generating thoughts
for the purpose of preserving the ego-mind
from the time a human wakes up the morning
until a human goes to sleep at night.
Reading one of those five books **every day**
puts a new stream of thought into the mind
that is countering those ego preservation thoughts.

2. In order to stay on this
New Unique Direct Path to Manonasa
you have to understand this Path.
Reading one of those five books **every day**
helps to keep your understanding of this Path
fresh in mind.

3. Reading one of those five books **every day**
provides encouragement and motivation to practice
and to stay on this
New Unique Direct Path to Manonasa.

4. Reading one of those five books **every day**
reminds you of why you are practicing
the Most Direct and Rapid Means to Manonasa
and why you chose this
New Unique Direct Path to Manonasa
instead of some other path.

Those rare one in a million spiritual seekers
in whom their desire to end the ego illusion
is greater than their desire to continue the ego illusion
who become aware of this
New Unique Direct Path to Manonasa
will prefer this **New Unique** Path to Manonasa
to all other Paths.

They will be able to see the unique value of this path.

THE UNIQUE VALUE OF THIS **NEW UNIQUE** DIRECT PATH TO MANONASA

A few hours before Yogi Kanna's body life came to an end, Yogi Kanna thanked me for this work and Yogi Kanna wished that when he is reborn that he would find these Teachings again.
Yogi Kanna had more than 11 years experience with these teachings.
These teachings brought Yogi Kanna to the doorway to Manonasa.
Not even one in ten million humans ever reaches the doorway to Manonasa.
Once someone reaches the doorway to Manonasa it is up to them to choose to go trough that doorway or to choose not to go through that doorway.
It is not up to me.
Yogi Kanna only averaged around two hours practice per day.
Much more would have been possible with more practice.
Yogi Kanna's example of wishing to find these teachings in his next life may help you see why protecting these teachings for thousands of years is one of my missions.

That one in a million spiritual seeker who would like to attain Manonasa, Nirvana, Self-Realization without delay, who is being honest with themselves about that and not lying to themselves about that, will recognize the unique value of this **New Unique** Direct Path to Manonasa, Nirvana, Self Realization.
Such a rare seeker will never want to try to study and practice teachings in which the reflection of the foolish thoughts of the questioner have not been removed.

In order for you to see the Unique Value
of this **New Unique** Direct Path to Manonasa
that is described in the 20 steps to Manonasa
at the end of this book
ponder these points:

1. The five books and this
New Unique Direct Path to Manonasa
were created by one who attained Manonasa.

Here is a quote by Ramana Maharshi:

"**By him alone whose saved himself
can other folk be freed.
The help of others is as if
the blind the blind would lead**."

2. In the five books
the reflections of the foolish thoughts of the questioner
were **not** included.
In other sources of the Direct Path Sages teachings,
the reflections of the foolish thoughts of the questioner
were included
and with a 700 page book for example
the reflections of the foolish thoughts of the questioner
are more than 500 of the 700 pages.
Ramana Maharshi has pointed out in quote #34
from *The Seven Steps to Awakening*
that it is a mistake to consider
the reflections of the foolish thoughts
of those who come before the Sage
as the Sage's thoughts even if the Sage said them.

3. Only the most essential points
needed for attaining Manonasa
were included in the five books.

STOP!

If you wonder about the harsh criticism
I have stated that is directed towards
all of the more than 6 billion humans on the earth,
here is an illustration that can help you to understand:

Let us suppose that you see a child
who is about to cross the street.
The child has not looked both ways before crossing
and the child does not see that a car is approaching
very rapidly.
You are not standing close enough to the child to grab
the child and to stop the child from crossing the street.
If you do not do something the child is going to be hit
by that car and the child's body life will come to an end.
What you must do is to shout as loud as you can:

STOP!

The child is not even looking at you
and if you speak softly the child may not hear you
or may think you are talking to someone else.
If you speak softly the child may be hit by the car
and the child's bodily life will come to an end.

The more than 6 billion human beings on earth
are making a choice not to attain Manonasa.
In their future
8,000,000,000,000,000,000,000,000,000
imaginary lifetimes they are going to experience
the equivalent of 4,000,000,000,000,000,000
oceans of suffering and sorrow.

If they follow any of the spiritual teachings of the past
they are **not** going to attain Manonasa
and they are going to experience
all those future lifetimes
with all that suffering and sorrow.
The ego-mind-thought, is a parasite that has no value
and is the source of all evil.
If humans follow any of the spiritual teachings
of the past that ego-mind-thought-evil
and the sorrow and suffering will continue.
If they follow no spiritual path
the same suffering will continue.

I know that the ego will **not** allow most people
to see that all the spiritual teachings of the past
were either created by the ego-mind
or immediately changed by the ego-mind
to serve the ego-mind.
I know that most humans will **not** be able to see
that the ego-mind is 100% evil.
I know that most humans will **not** be able to see
that the ego-mind lies to its imaginary self
from the time it wakes up in the morning
until it goes to sleep at night.

This book is written for those few
whose ego-mind will allow them to see
at least a little bit of what this book is trying to convey.
For most people the ego-mind
is **not** going to allow them to see
even a little bit of what this book is trying to convey.

It might be possible for you the reader to see that
in spite of all the religious and spiritual paths
of the past, humans are stuck.
Humans are **not** being freed by the
spiritual and religious teachings of the past.

For the same reason that
you must **shout** as loud as you can
to stop that child from crossing the street
who is not within your reach
to prevent that child from being hit by the car,
in order to prevent as many humans as possible
from continuing the evil ego illusion
and having to go through
8,000,000,000,000,000,000,000,000,000
future imaginary lifetimes
and having to experience in those future lifetimes
the equivalent of 4,000,000,000,000,000,000
oceans of suffering and sorrow,
I am saying to humanity:

STOP!

Remember these 9 reasons why all of the spiritual teachings of the past are leading to ego preservation and not to ego dissolution:

1. Most of the spiritual teachings of the past
were created by people
in whom the ego illusion had not ended
and therefore from the beginning
the purpose of the spiritual teaching
was to preserve the ego illusion
even if the teaching pretended to be
for the purpose of ending the ego illusion.

2. Those very few spiritual teachings that were created
by one in whom the ego illusion had ended
were distorted immediately and changed into a teaching
that preserves the ego illusion
and that will **never** bring the ego illusion to a final end.

3. The spiritual teachings of the past
are distractions and detours,
nothing more.

4. The spiritual teachings of the past
are **not** steps to Awakening.

5. The purpose of the spiritual teachings of the past
is to **prevent** you from awakening
from the human dream.

6. The spiritual teachings of the past
will **never** bring suffering to a final end.

7. The spiritual teachings of the past
will **never** lead you to Eternal Bliss.

8. All of the six billion humans on the earth are a lie.
The spiritual teachings of the past are a part of that lie.

9. Humanity has been caught in the same ego trap
for all of human history.
The spiritual teachings of the past
are part of that ego trap.

The reason for my harsh criticism of humanity
has been explained above
including the example of the child
who is about to get hit by a car
and the only way to prevent that is to **shout** STOP!

In the case of my core students
the approach is different.
I do not criticize them.
I give them my unconditional love and encouragement.
They have made the decision
to bring the ego-mind to a final end.

Going back to the example of the child
who was about to cross the street.
The child heard you **shout** stop and the child stopped.
At that point it is very important
that you do **not** continue to shout at the child.
If you shouted at the child at that point
you could scare the child
so that the child ran into the road and got hit by a car.

The 20 Steps to Manonasa that follow
are a new spiritual path.
It is a **New Unique** Direct Path to Manonasa
that unlike other paths
is **not** just claiming to be a direct path to Manonasa
while it is really serving the ego-mind.
The 20 steps to Manonasa
offers humanity an alternative
to the spiritual and religious teachings of the past.

It also offers humanity an alternative
to the false spiritual teachings
that will be created in the future.

THE **NEW UNIQUE** DIRECT PATH TO MANONASA

IS FOLLOWING THESE 20 STEPS.

20 STEPS TO MANONASA

If you would like to attain Manonasa
follow **all** of the following 20 steps:

Read the following five books cover to cover:

1. *The Seven Steps to Awakening.*

2. *The Direct Means to Eternal Bliss.*

3. *How To Practice the Teachings.*

4. *Manonasa: A Spiritual Autobiography.*

5. *Experience Your Perfect Soul.*

6. At seeseer.com click the “Free” Tab.
Then click the Self Awareness Practice Instructions playlist link. Then add that link to your favorites or bookmark that link
or put that link where you will be able to find it easily.

7. Click the link for the Eternal Bliss Group.
Join the Eternal Bliss Group.

8. On the Self Awareness Practice Instructions youtube video playlist watch the video
titled Self Awareness and the Heart.
Every time you are going to practice Self Awareness watch and listen to one or two of the songs
on one of the four music playlists
per the instructions
on the Self Awareness and the Heart video.

9. Watch all of the videos on the
Self Awareness Practice Instructions
youtube video playlist.

10. Every day drop all of your unnecessary activities and spend ½ of the free time thus created
practicing the Awareness Watching Awareness Method as described in the book *The Direct Means to Eternal Bliss* or Self Awareness as described in the
Self Awareness Practice Instructions videos
or as described in the Step Seven Quotes in the book *The Seven Steps to Awakening*.
Instead of practicing AWA or Self Awareness,
if you prefer, you can practice the Loving Consciousness Method or the Abandon Release Method as described in the book *The Direct Means to Eternal Bliss*.
If you choose to practice the Loving Consciousness Method, every day read the quotes in the book
How to Live a Life that Knows Only Love.

11. Spend the other ½ of the free time thus created
reading or rereading one of the five books
named at the beginning of this list of steps.

12. Follow the suggestions in the book
The Direct Means to Eternal Bliss for how to awaken
the extremely intense desire for freedom.
i.e. facing the negative,
remembering how short and temporary human life is,
reading the Step Five quotes in
The Seven Steps to Awakening.

13. Do not limit yourself just to the suggestions
in the book *The Direct Means to Eternal Bliss* for how
to Awaken the Extremely Intense Desire for Liberation.
Experiment and find out
what will increase your desire for Liberation
until that desire has the energy of a trillion stars.
The most important key for attaining Manonasa
is the intensity of your desire for Liberation.
Compared to that all other keys to Manonasa
are like comparing the light of a light bulb
to the light of the sun.
The intensity of your desire for liberation
is like the light of the sun.
All other keys to Manonasa
are like the light of a light bulb.

14. Catch your ego lying to you every day.
Catch your ego trying to lead you away from this
New Unique Direct Path to Manonasa.
Catch your ego trying to have you waste time
in unnecessary activities.

15. Practice the 5 steps for the Majority
that you will see at the very end of this autobiography.

16. Never cause any type of harm to a human being
or an animal.

17. In order for the five books listed
at the top of this list to penetrate the thousands of layers
of human self deception
that are called the human mind,
and so that the teachings are so well placed in memory
that the teachings become tools you can use,
read all five books hundreds of times cover to cover.

18. With every paragraph you read in those five books
ask yourself how can I put this into practice?
Then write down on a piece of paper or digitally
the answers to that question.
What you have written down
are your practice instructions.

19. Read one of the practice instructions mentioned
in step #18 at least 40 times per day every day
spread throughout your waking hours and then
ACTUALLY PUT THE INSTRUCTION
INTO PRACTICE.
The next day read a different practice instruction
and follow the instructions listed here in step #19
using that different instruction.
Continue that pattern every day.

20. If you want to read more spiritual books in addition to the five at the top of this 20 steps list, read these 8 books:

1. *The True Self.*

2. *The Importance of Practice & Effort.*

3. *How to Practice Self Inquiry.*

4. *Contemplating Who Am I?*

5. *How to Live a Life That Knows Only Love.*

6. *Self Abidance, Abridged Edition.*

7. *Powerful Quotes from Sankara.*

8. *Powerful Buddhist Quotes.*

For more information about those books go to:

www.seeseer.com

FIVE STEPS FOR THE MAJORITY

For those of you
who do not want to attain Manonasa
but you would like to know
how you can move from darkness to light
follow all 5 steps on this page every day.
All of you who do want to attain Manonasa
should also follow the suggestions on this page
because these suggestions are for all of
the more than 6 billion humans on earth:

1. Every time you speak to a human being
either in person or over the phone,
make sure the content of what you are saying
and the tone of your voice are loving, caring, and kind.

2. Every time you write something to a human being
make sure that what you are writing is loving and kind.
Pause before you send someone an email
or a text message and make sure that your email
or text message is loving, caring and kind.

3. Never do any harm of any kind to any human being
or animal.

4. Treat even the people who you think
do not deserve your kindness with kindness.

5. Treat even people you only see briefly
with great caring and kindness.

ʒ

Made in the USA
Las Vegas, NV
26 April 2021

22019594R00138